ENGLISH

Curriculum Bank

KEY STAGE TWO
SCOTTISH LEVELS C-E

WRITING

DAVID WAUGH WITH NICK McGUINN

Published by Scholastic Ltd,
Villiers House,
Clarendon Avenue,
Leamington Spa,
Warwickshire CV32 5PR
Text © David Waugh and Nick McGuinn
© 1996 Scholastic Ltd
67890   89012345

AUTHORS
DAVID WAUGH WITH NICK McGUINN

EDITOR
CLARE GALLAHER

ASSISTANT EDITOR
KATE PEARCE

SERIES DESIGNER
LYNNE JOESBURY

DESIGNER
ANNA OLIWA

ILLUSTRATIONS
PETER STEVENSON

COVER ILLUSTRATION
JONATHAN BENTLEY

INFORMATION TECHNOLOGY CONSULTANT
MARTIN BLOWS

SCOTTISH 5–14 LINKS
MARGARET SCOTT AND SUSAN GOW

Designed using Adobe Pagemaker

British Library Cataloguing-in-Publication Data
A catalogue record for this book is available from the
British Library.

ISBN 0-590-53399-1

Contents

ACKNOWLEDGEMENTS

The authors would like to thank Rosemary Waugh, a teacher at Kingston High School, Hull; John Addison, a teacher at Hollin Primary School in Middleton, Manchester; and Ann Addison, Headteacher at Hill Top Primary School, Rochdale for their help with ideas for this book.

The publishers gratefully acknowledge permission to reproduce the following copyright material:

Hodder Headline for an extract from *The Linc Reader* edited by Ron Carter © 1990 Ron Carter (Hodder and Stoughton,1990); Moira .Andrew for an extract from 'Sleeping Cats' by Moira Andrew © 1992 Moira Andrew from *Scholastic Collections Poetry* (Scholastic Ltd, 1992); Bloodaxe Books Ltd for an extract from 'For F.E.H.' by Frances Horovitz © 1985 Frances Horovitz from *Collected Poems* (Bloodaxe, 1985); Celia Warren for an extract from 'Aeroplane' by Celia Warren © 1992 Celia Warren from *Scholastic Collections Poetry* (Scholastic Ltd, 1992); John Rice for previously unpublished extract from the poem 'A Gift from the Stars' © 1996 John Rice.

Introduction

Scholastic Curriculum Bank is a series for all primary teachers, providing an essential planning tool for devising comprehensive schemes of work as well as an easily accessible and varied bank of practical, classroom-tested activities with photocopiable resources.

Designed to help planning for and implementation of progression, differentiation and assessment, *Scholastic Curriculum Bank* offers a structured range of stimulating activities with clearly stated learning objectives that reflect the programmes of study, and detailed lesson plans that allow busy teachers to put ideas into practice with the minimum amount of preparation time. The photocopiable sheets that accompany many of the activities provide ways of integrating purposeful application of knowledge and skills, differentiation, assessment and record-keeping.

Opportunities for formative assessment are highlighted within the activities where appropriate, while separate summative assessment activities give guidelines for analysis and subsequent action. Ways of using information technology for different purposes and in different contexts, as a tool for communicating and handling information and as a means of investigating, are integrated into the activities where appropriate, and more explicit guidance is provided at the end of the book.

The series covers all the primary curriculum subjects, with separate books for Key Stages 1 and 2 or Scottish Levels A–B and C–E. It can be used as a flexible resource with any scheme, to fulfil National Curriculum and Scottish 5–14 requirements and to provide children with a variety of different learning experiences that will lead to effective acquisition of skills and knowledge.

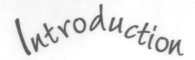
SCHOLASTIC CURRICULUM BANK ENGLISH

The *Scholastic Curriculum Bank English* books enable teachers to plan comprehensive and structured coverage of the primary English curriculum, and enable pupils to develop the required skills, knowledge and understanding through activities.

Each book contains one key stage. There are four books for Key Stage 1/Scottish levels A–B and four for Key Stage 2/Scottish levels C–E. These books reflect the English Programme of Study, so that there are titles on Reading, Writing, Speaking and listening and Spelling and phonics.

Bank of activities
This book provides a bank of activities which are designed to broaden children's experience of writing and enable them to develop their abilities to communicate clearly and accurately through writing.

Lesson plans
Detailed lesson plans, under clear headings, are given for each activity and provide material for immediate implementation in the classroom. The structure for each activity is as follows.

Activity title box
The information contained in the box at the beginning of each activity outlines the following key aspects:
▲ *Activity title and learning objective.* For each activity a clearly stated learning objective is given in bold italics. These

learning objectives break down aspects of the programmes of study into manageable, hierarchical teaching and learning chunks, and their purpose is to aid planning for progression. These objectives can be easily referenced to the National Curriculum and Scottish 5–14 requirements by using the overview grids at the end of this chapter (pages 9 to 14).
▲ *Class organisation/Likely duration.* Icons ✝✝ and 🕐 signpost the suggested group sizes for each activity and the approximate amount of time required to complete it.

Previous skills/knowledge needed
Information is given here when it is necessary for the children to have acquired specific knowledge or skills prior to carrying out the activity.

Key background information
The information in this section outlines the areas of study covered by each activity and gives a general background to the particular topic or theme, outlining the basic skills that will be developed and the way in which the activity will address children's learning.

Preparation
Advice is given for those occasions where it is necessary for the teacher to prime the pupils for the activity or to prepare materials, or to set up a display or activity ahead of time.

Resources needed
All of the materials needed to carry out the activity are listed, so that the pupils or the teacher can gather them together easily before the beginning of the teaching session.

Introduction

What to do

Easy-to-follow, step-by-step instructions are given for carrying out the activity, including (where appropriate) suggested questions for the teacher to ask pupils to help instigate discussion and stimulate investigation.

Suggestion(s) for extension/support

Ideas are given for ways of providing easy differentiation where activities lend themselves to this purpose. In all cases, suggestions are provided as to ways in which each activity can be modified for less able or extended for more able children.

Assessment opportunities

Where appropriate, opportunities for ongoing teacher assessment of the children's work during or after a specific activity are highlighted.

Opportunities for IT

Where opportunities for IT present themselves, these are briefly outlined with reference to particularly suitable types of program. The chart on page 158 presents specific areas of IT covered in the activities, together with more detailed support on how to apply particular types of program. Selected lesson plans serve as models for other activities by providing more comprehensive guidance on the application of IT, and these are indicated by the bold page numbers on the grid and the  icon at the start of an activity.

Display ideas

Where they are relevant and innovative, display ideas are incorporated into activity plans and illustrated with examples.

Other aspects of the English PoS covered

Inevitably, as all areas of English are interrelated, activities will cover aspects of the programmes of study in other areas of the English curriculum. These links are highlighted under this heading.

Reference to photocopiable sheets

Where activities include photocopiable activity sheets, small reproductions of these are included in the lesson plans together with guidance notes for their use and, where appropriate, suggested answers.

Assessment

In this book, advice is given for each activity on what the teacher should look out for during the course of the activity. Notes made on individual children's progress may contribute to an overall profile of each child which could include samples of writing in various genres.

At the end of each chapter there is an activity which is designed to provide a summative measure of a range of key competencies linked to the type of writing dealt with in that chapter. This activity is similar in its organisation to the preceding ones, and focuses on a number of learning objectives covered in the chapter. Assessment activities are indicated by the icon.

Photocopiable activity sheets

Many of the activities are accompanied by photocopiable activity sheets. For some activities, there may be more than one version; or an activity sheet may be 'generic', with a facility for the teacher to fill in the appropriate task in order to provide differentiation by task. Other sheets may be more

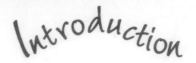

open-ended to provide differentiation by outcome. The photocopiable activity sheets provide purposeful activities that are ideal for assessment and can be kept as records in pupils' portfolios of work.

Cross-curricular links

Cross-curricular links are identified on a simple grid which cross-references the particular areas of study in English to the programmes of study for other subjects in the curriculum, and where appropriate provides suggestions for activities (see page 160).

WRITING

This book is intended to help teachers to fulfil the National Curriculum requirement that at Key Stage 2, children 'should be given opportunities to write for varied purposes, understanding that writing is essential to thinking and learning, and enjoyable in itself'.

Throughout the book it is emphasised that writing is a means of communication and, as such, demands that a range of real 'audiences' is provided so that children see the activity as purposeful. A wide variety of genres is provided so that children will have opportunities to experience various literary forms and develop appropriate styles.

Many of the activities involve children in drafting their work. Through planning, revising and proofreading their writing, children can come to see that writing can be temporary and can be changed to improve both presentation and style. In determining which activities might involve drafting, careful consideration has been given to the nature of the activities

and the ways in which children's work will subsequently be celebrated.

An important element of the book is the attention given to developing children's knowledge about language. There is a popular belief that this area of English has been neglected in the past and that a return to grammatical exercises would lead to an improvement in children's writing. The activities presented here do include some exercises designed to reinforce learning, but the exercises should not be used as a substitute for teaching and learning. Wherever exercises are used it is hoped that teachers will enable children to view them as purposeful and see them in the context of other learning. The development of knowledge about language is important as it provides a greater understanding of the ways in which language can be used and opens up possibilities in children's writing. For example, an understanding of the use of pronouns can allow children to vary the vocabulary of their writing and avoid repeated use of proper nouns. This book attempts to raise awareness of literary devices such as similes, adjectives and adverbs and through doing so aims to foster the development of a metalanguage through which children may discuss their writing.

The National Writing Project's book *Perceptions of Writing* (Nelson, 1989) showed that, for many children, writing is regarded as a chore. Some felt that they were being asked to write so that the teacher could mark spellings, punctuation or handwriting. It is hoped that this book will afford teachers the opportunity to develop their pupils' skills in these important areas, but it is also hoped that other aspects of writing, such as language use, quality of content and vocabulary choice, will be accorded high status too.

Learning objective	PoS/AO	Content	Type of activity	Page
Chapter 1 – Imaginative writing				
To show an awareness of the features of report writing.	1a, c. *Functional writing: Level C.*	Looking at newspaper reporting and writing reports.	Individuals or pairs writing in response to a picture stimulus.	16
To demonstrate an understanding of drafting.	1a; 2b. *Imaginative writing: Level C.*	Developing writing in sentences.	Individual work based upon notes provided on photocopiable sheet.	17
To demonstrate an increased awareness of, and ability to use, the features of report writing.	1a, c. *Functional writing: Level C.*	Studying newspaper reporting as an introduction to report writing.	Report writing by individuals or pairs based upon headlines provided on photocopiable sheet.	18
To show an appreciation of ways of using planning and drafting to refine and develop writing.	1a; 2b. *Imaginative writing: Level C.*	Studying well-known sayings, morals and proverbs as a stimulus for writing.	Paired or individual work writing stories based on sayings, morals and proverbs.	20
To produce writing based upon careful observation.	1a, c. *Personal writing: Level C.*	Creative writing based on observation of the weather.	Individual work following note-making outdoors.	22
To produce imaginative writing developed through planning and drafting.	1a; 2b. *Personal writing: Level C.*	Chronological writing based on close observation.	Individual creative writing based on stimulus of looking at and eating a Smartie.	22
To produce imaginative writing based on research.	1a, c. *Functional writing: Level C.*	Looking at examples of interviews in magazines, and children creating their own based on research.	Class or group reading, leading to writing in an interview format, either individually or in pairs.	24
To write for an audience.	1a, b, c. *Functional writing: Level C.*	Communication without talking.	Pairs writing notes to each other.	25
To demonstrate an awareness of the features and importance of the opening paragraph of a story.	1a; 2b. *Imaginative writing: Level D.*	Looking at examples of opening paragraphs to stories.	Writing opening paragraphs for a story following a structured introduction.	26
To produce co-operative writing based upon drafting, revising and editing.	1a; 2b. *Personal writing: Level D.*	Note-making based on stimulating pictures being passed around the group.	Following note-making and sharing of ideas, children work in pairs to produce a piece of descriptive poetry or prose.	28
To write in response to a stimulus and to create and describe a character.	1a, c. *Imaginative writing: Level C.*	Examination of contents of a mystery wallet followed by discussion and writing.	Individual or paired descriptive writing about the character who might have owned a mystery wallet.	29
To produce imaginative writing developed through planning and drafting.	1a; 2b. *Imaginative writing: Level C.*	Reading well-known stories and considering what might become of the main characters.	Writing individually or in pairs about the future life of a well-known fictional character.	30
To write in response to a stimulus and to develop awareness of a variety of outcomes for a story.	1a, c. *Imaginative writing: Level C.*	Discussing genre of stories in which the reader can influence the outcome by throwing a die.	Paired writing using a die to determine which of a range of possible directions a story takes.	31
To produce imaginative writing developed through planning and drafting.	1a; 2b. *Imaginative writing: Level C.*	Discussion of stories in which characters enter other worlds.	Individual writing of stories in which characters enter other worlds.	32

WRITING

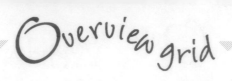

Learning objective	PoS/AO	Content	Type of activity	Page
To show an awareness of writing for the needs of a particular range of readers, using appropriate vocabulary and style.	1a, b. *Imaginative writing: Level C.*	Discussion of stories about mythical creatures and about ways of making stories appropriate for a younger age group.	Individuals or pairs writing stories and possibly producing booklets.	33
To show an appreciation of range of genre and an ability to produce imaginative, drafted writing.	1a, c. *Imaginative writing: Level C.*	Reading and listening to cautionary tales and discussion.	Individuals or pairs drafting cautionary stories.	34
To demonstrate an ability to edit and revise writing to make it more concise.	1a; 2b. *Imaginative writing: Level D.*	Discussion of mini sagas and concise use of words.	Individuals or pairs working to produce concise pieces of writing with a prescribed number of words.	35
To demonstrate an awareness of writing for a particular audience, using appropriate vocabulary and style.	1a, b. *Imaginative writing: Level C.*	Discussion and reading of well-known nursery stories and fairy tales.	Individuals or pairs planning and writing their own versions of well-known nursery stories.	36
To show an ability to write in an extended range of genre.	1a, c. *Functional writing: Level C.*	Reading examples of horoscopes and discussing content.	Individuals and small groups writing horoscopes.	37
To write in response to a particular stimulus.	1a; 2a. *Imaginative writing: Level C.*	Investigating features and habits of different animals.	Individuals writing from the point of view of animals.	38
To show an ability to produce imaginative, speculative writing.	1a; 2a. *Personal writing: Level C.*	Discussing what children would do if they suddenly became rich.	Individuals writing about what they would do if they acquired a lot of money.	39
To demonstrate greater understanding of writing for a range of audiences and improvement in presentational skills.	1a, b. *Imaginative writing/ Presentation: Level C.*	Looking at Mr Men books by Roger Hargreaves and discussing style and genre.	Individuals or pairs writing Mr Men stories.	40
To demonstrate an ability to use adjectives, nouns and verbs in poetic writing.	1a; 3b. *Personal writing: Level C.*	Class or group work on parts of speech and their roles.	Whole class or group poetry writing.	41
To use the features of rhyming poetry to write for a real audience.	1a, b; 2a. *Personal writing: Level C.*	Studying greetings cards and the poems and verses inside them.	Individuals or pairs writing verses for greetings cards and making cards.	43
To show an awareness of and ability to use poetic structure and rhyme.	1a, b, c. *Personal writing: Level C.*	Reading and listening to limericks and discussing their format and the nature of rhymes and syllables.	Individuals or pairs writing limericks.	44
To demonstrate an increased awareness of the poetic form.	1a, c. *Personal writing: Level C.*	Studying hymns, their words, meanings and structures.	Pairs writing alternative lyrics for hymns.	45
To show a greater understanding of range of genre.	1a, b, c. *Personal writing: Level C.*	Looking at and discussing a variety of prayers.	Children writing prayers individually or in pairs.	46
To use a well-defined poetic structure.	1a, b, c. *Personal writing: Level D.*	Studying haiku and discussing syllables and concise writing.	Children working individually to write haiku.	46
To write poetry within a structured scheme.	1a, b, c. *Personal writing: Level C.*	Reading and discussing 'No!' by Thomas Hood.	Individuals or pairs writing poems in which the first word is the same for each line.	47

WRITING

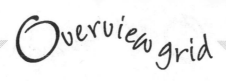

Learning objective	PoS/AO	Content	Type of activity	Page
To write imaginatively in a structured form.	1a, b, c; 2a, b, c, d, e; 3a, b, c. *Personal writing: Level C.*	Listening to and discussing poem.	Children writing poems individually.	48
Chapter 2 – Non-fiction writing				
To use notes as a starting point for writing in prose.	1a, b; 2b. *Functional writing: Level C.*	Discussing telegram format and interpreting messages in greater detail.	Individuals or pairs rewriting telegram messages in sentences.	50
To record information concisely and accurately.	1a, c. *Functional writing: Level C.*	Researching interesting facts following reading of an excerpt from *Danny, the Champion of the World* by Roald Dahl.	Individuals or pairs writing interesting facts for display at various times.	51
To demonstrate awareness of the importance of layout and presentation and an ability to use some features to present work attractively.	1a, c. *Functional writing/ Presentation: Level D.*	Discussion of book covers and the ways in which they are designed to encourage readership.	Children examine book covers and then produce their own, individually or in pairs.	52
To show understanding of the features of instructional writing and an ability to use these.	1a, b, c. *Functional writing: Level D.*	Discussion of recipe format.	Children find recipes from home and write them in their own words.	53
To write in response to a stimulus.	1a, b, c. *Personal writing: Level C.*	Discussion of New Year's resolutions.	Children work individually to write their New Year's resolutions.	54
To use adjectives to improve descriptive writing.	1a; 2a. *Imaginative writing: Level C.*	Making a character web of a chosen person.	Individuals work on descriptive writing.	54
To use the features of descriptive writing in response to a stimulus.	1a; 2a. *Functional writing: Level C.*	Studying and discussing pictures and plans of rooms.	Individual descriptions of children's ideal rooms.	55
To make use of revising and drafting as a starting point for preparing a verbal presentation.	1a; 2b. *Functional writing: Level D.*	Discussing presentations and ways of planning for them.	Children working individually or in pairs to research and prepare a talk to the class.	56
To communicate ideas in writing.	1a, b. *Functional writing: Level C.*	Discussing rules and ways in which they might be written down.	Children working in pairs or small groups to write rules for the class which may then be discussed and incorporated into a set of rules produced by the whole class.	57
To use an appropriate vocabulary and style of writing for a particular audience.	1a, b. *Functional writing: Level C.*	Discussing postcards and the concise nature of information given on them.	Children make their own postcards and write messages on them.	58
To use the features of layout and presentation of a flow chart.	1a; 2b. *Functional writing: Level C.*	Discussion of flow charts, their layout and purpose.	Children work individually or in pairs to produce flow charts for familiar activities.	59
To write for a real audience of parents and visitors to the school.	1a, b. *Functional writing: Level C.*	Discussing programmes for a variety of events.	Small groups or pairs producing programmes for a school event.	60
To write in the style of a journal.	1a, b, c. *Personal writing: Level C.*	Discussing diaries and their layout and style.	Individuals writing diary entries at various times throughout one day.	61

WRITING

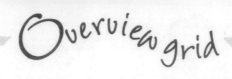

Learning objective	PoS/AO	Content	Type of activity	Page
To write questions related to the reading of books.	1a, c. *Functional writing: Level C.*	Discussing questions one might ask about a book.	Children work individually as part of an ongoing activity to write questions about the books they read.	62
To use the features of layout and presentation of a questionnaire.	1a, c. *Functional writing: Level D.*	Discussing sample questionnaires and the general purpose of questionnaires.	Children work individually to complete questionnaires.	63
To produce accurate non-fiction writing in an appropriate style.	1a, b, c; 2a, b, c, d, e; 3a, b, c. *Functional writing: Level C.*	Researching and discussing playground games.	Children writing about games individually.	64
Chapter 3 – Language study				
To use full stops accurately.	2c. *Punctuation and structure: Level B.*	Discussing the nature of sentences and the need for punctuation.	A walking and reading exercise followed by children discussing the placement of full stops in an unpunctuated passage.	66
To produce a bank of four-letter words which are spelled correctly.	2d. *Spelling: Level B. Knowledge about language: Level C.*	Collecting as many four-letter words as possible using dictionaries and other books.	Individuals or pairs using four-letter words in a piece of writing.	67
To make use of conjunctions to link sentences.	3b. *Knowledge about language: Level D.*	Discussing ways of combining short sentences to make longer ones.	Individuals or pairs working from photocopiable sheet to combine sentences.	68
To demonstrate an understanding of sentence structure.	3b. *Knowledge about language: Level B.*	Discussing incomplete sentences and the nature of sentences.	Children work individually or in pairs to finish incomplete sentences provided on photocopiable sheet.	69
To use question marks accurately.	2c. *Knowledge about language: Level C.*	Playing various games to aid understanding of direct and indirect questions.	Children asking direct and indirect questions to each other and writing questions to go with answers provided on photocopiable sheet.	70
To use commas correctly in sentences.	2c. *Punctuation/ Knowledge about language: Level C.*	Discussing the importance of the comma and telling the story of 'The comma that saved a human life'.	Working in small groups to put commas in sentences on photocopiable sheet.	72
To use exclamation marks appropriately.	2c. *Punctuation/ Knowledge about language: Level C.*	Sitting in a circle and passing words round which require exclamation, followed by scripting of radio plays.	Small groups writing scripts for short plays which include exclamations.	73
To use speech marks accurately.	2c. *Punctuation/ Knowledge about language: Level D.*	Studying comics and speech bubbles and discussing the way in which speech should be written in reported speech.	Individuals transcribing speech from speech bubbles into reported speech.	75
To use paragraphs accurately.	3b. *Punctuation and Structure: Level D.*	Discussing paragraphs and why they are used.	Children working in small groups on the paragraphs provided on photocopiable sheet.	76

Learning objective	PoS/AO	Content	Type of activity	Page
To use pronouns appropriately to enhance writing.	3b. *Knowledge about language: Level D.*	Discussing example from photocopiable sheet and eliciting from children that pronouns might make it more interesting and less repetitive.	Children writing in small groups, pairs or individually about a friend or relative, using pronouns as often as possible.	77
To write clear definitions of words.	3a. *Functional writing: Level D.*	Using dictionaries to find unusual words and discussing definitions.	Small groups writing definitions for words, some of which are false, and then playing game.	78
To understand how written standard English often differs from spoken dialect.	3a. *Knowledge about language: Level D.*	Listening to and discussing examples of different dialects.	Whole class, individuals or pairs rewriting dialect texts in standard English.	79
To understand how written standard English often differs from spoken dialect.	3a. *Knowledge about language: Level D.*	Discussing dialect words and the places where they are used.	Small groups interviewing members of staff or other volunteers and recording origins of dialect words on a map.	81
To use apostrophes for abbreviation accurately.	2c. *Punctuation/ Knowledge about language: Level E.*	Discussing the use of apostrophes for abbreviation.	Individuals working from photocopiable sheets.	83
To use apostrophes to show possession accurately.	2c. *Punctuation/ Knowledge about language: Level E.*	Studying examples of the use of apostrophes to indicate possession.	Writing short story or sentences using apostrophes to denote possession. Working from photocopiable sheet.	84
To understand that complex sentences are divided into clauses and phrases.	1a; 3b. *Knowledge about language: Level E.*	Discussing the use of clauses and phrases and talking about examples.	Children writing phrases and clauses to a main independent clause to write opening lines for different types of story.	85
To show understanding of the principal parts of speech.	3b. *Knowledge about language: Level D.*	Discussing nonsense sentences.	Children writing nonsense sentences following a set pattern.	87
To use adjectives effectively to enhance writing.	3b. *Knowledge about language: Level D.*	Discussing the use of adjectives in prose and poetry.	Children adding adjectives to bland passages to make them more interesting.	88
To understand and make use of similes.	1a; 3c. *Knowledge about language: Level E.*	Discussing figurative language in poetry or prose.	Individuals adding similes to extracts from poems and comparing these with the original versions.	89
To understand and use onomatopoeic words in writing.	1a; 3c. *Knowledge about language: Level E.*	Discussing onomatopoeic words and their functions.	Children adding onomatopoeic words to a passage on photocopiable sheet and then writing their own passages including such words.	91
To demonstrate an ability to edit and to write concisely.	2b. *Functional writing: Level E.*	Whole class or group working with the teacher to reduce the number of words in a passage presented on photocopiable sheet.	Children working individually within groups to write passages which are passed on and made more concise.	92
To be able to present text which has been read in one genre in a different form.	1a; 2c. *Punctuation: Level D.*	Discussing the layout of drama scripts.	Children working from photocopiable sheet to rewrite scripts in prose.	93

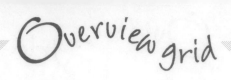

Learning objective	PoS/AO	Content	Type of activity	Page
To write sentences which begin with adverbs.	3b. *Punctuation and Structure: Level D.*	Discussing sentences beginning with adverbs and in particular those beginning with 'fortunately' or 'unfortunately'.	Children writing individually within groups or pairs, writing sentences beginning with 'fortunately' and 'unfortunately'.	95
To use the features of standard written English, including the use of accurate punctuation and spelling and a range of parts of speech, to enhance the quality of writing.	1a, b, c; 2a, b, c, d, e; 3a, b, c. *Functional writing: Level D.*	Reading and discussing newspaper reports.	Children writing reports individually.	96
Chapter 4 – Persuasive writing				
To use writing persuasively.	1a, b, c. *Functional writing: Level D.*	Discussing fact and opinion and relating this to an advertisement on photocopiable sheet.	Children analysing and then responding to an advertisement's factual inaccuracies.	98
To produce instructional writing.	1a, b, c. *Functional writing: Level C.*	Discussing labels of various products and the directions provided on them.	Individuals or pairs produce their own labels for imaginary products.	99
To present coherent arguments in written form.	1b, c. *Functional writing: Level D.*	Discussing Alan Ahlberg's poem 'It's not Fair' and talking about things which the children feel are unfair.	Children working individually or in pairs to write about things that they find unfair.	100
To write for a range of audiences.	1a, b, c; 2a, e. *Functional writing/ Presentation: Level D.*	Discussing the qualities of guidebooks.	Children, in pairs or small groups, producing guidebooks for the school.	101
To write to communicate ideas.	1a, b, c. *Functional writing: Level C.*	Discussing the characteristics of various celebrities.	Children make lists of their favourite celebrities and write sentences justifying their choices.	102
To write in an appropriate style for an extended range of readers.	1a, b, c; 3a. *Functional writing: Level D.*	Studying job advertisements and discussing ways of applying for jobs.	Children writing formal letters 'applying' for jobs.	104
To use letter writing for an extended range of readers.	1a, b, c; 3a. *Functional writing: Level D.*	Discussing examples of problems and solutions from magazines and from photocopiable sheet.	Children working individually or in pairs to write solutions to problems provided on photocopiable sheet.	105
To write persuasively.	1a, b, c. *Functional writing: Level D.*	Considering favourite pieces of music and writing reasons for those choices.	Children working individually to write choices and explanations.	106
To write in a style appropriate for justifying choices.	1a, b, c. *Functional writing: Level D.*	Discussing a well-known book and the actors the children would choose to play the parts of different characters if a film were to be made.	Children working in pairs to cast a film and write justifications for their choices.	108
To write concisely and in a style appropriate for a classified ad.	1a, b, c; 2a. *Functional writing: Level D.*	Discussing examples of classified ads.	Children working in pairs to write their own classified ads.	109
To write persuasively.	1a, b, c; 2a, b, c, d, e; 3a, b, c. *Functional writing: Level E.*	Looking at and discussing letter columns in newspapers.	Children writing letters individually about an issue which concerns them.	110

Entries given in italics relate to the Scottish 5–14 Guidelines for English Language.

WRITING

Imaginative writing

In this chapter a variety of stimuli is suggested to encourage imaginative writing. There is a strong emphasis on the importance of children recognising a purpose for their writing and having a real audience to read it.

Some of the activities require individual work, but the majority may be attempted by pairs of children working collaboratively.

It is important that children's imaginative writing should be valued and that teachers' responses to it should not be dominated by attention to presentational aspects. Those children who experience difficulties with spelling and handwriting may make use of word processors in order to enable them to produce well-presented work.

In order to achieve good results, children will need to experience a range of literary genres and be exposed to these both through their personal reading and through having stories and poems read aloud to them. They will also need to develop a vocabulary with which to discuss their work. The use of terms such as 'adjective', 'adverb' and 'verb' should be encouraged in order to enable children to examine features of their own and other people's writing.

The activities range from poetry to story writing and include many which demand planning, drafting and editing. A key objective is to encourage children to regard themselves as real authors and learn the strategies which authors use.

15

INCIDENT IN THE PLAYGROUND

To show an awareness of the features of report writing.

†† *Individuals or pairs.*

🕐 *One hour.*

Key background information

This activity is designed to encourage children to look closely at a picture and think about the relationships between the people in it. It should promote report writing. 'Sometimes God' and 'Dog in the Playground' from Allan Ahlberg's *Please Mrs Butler* (Puffin, 1984) may prove excellent starting points for this activity.

Preparation

Cut out interesting action pictures from newspapers and magazines which show pictures of people. Make copies of photocopiable page 112, either one for each child or one per pair.

Resources needed

Pictures cut out of newspapers and magazines (see above), photocopiable page 112, A4 paper, pens, pencils.

What to do

First show the children examples of newspaper reports which have photographs accompanying them. Discuss the ways in which the reporters have interpreted events. For example, do they enable the reader to build up a picture of what happened and do they describe the part of the event which is featured in the photograph?

Next, show the children pictures of people cut from magazines and ask them what they think the people are

thinking about. Encourage them to look closely at the people's expressions. Ask them how they would report on the events in the picture.

Give out copies of photocopiable page 112 and tell the children to study the picture closely. Ask them to decide what each person is thinking and to write brief notes on this in the thought bubbles. When they have done this ask them to write a few sentences which provide greater detail, on a separate sheet of paper. They could try to write in the first person as if they were each of the characters or they could write as a newspaper reporter.

As the children are working, share their ideas and show examples of what they have written to the rest of the group. Encourage them to stop and discuss their different ideas.

Suggestion(s) for extension

The children could expand their ideas and develop their initial work into a story.

Suggestion(s) for support

Working in pairs, the children could list key words for their reports after they have used the photocopiable sheet and written notes in the thought bubbles. They could then be helped to put these into sentences.

Assessment opportunities

Note the children's abilities to use an appropriate style of writing for reporting. Note whether the style engages the interest of the reader and if it assumes that the reader was not present when the event took place.

Opportunities for IT

The children could use a word processor to write a newspaper style report for the action pictures which have been cut out of newspapers and magazines. If the school has a scanner, the pictures could be turned into digital images which could be used in a word processor or desktop publishing package, so that children's writing could be displayed alongside the picture. If it is not possible to scan the pictures, children could leave an appropriate space in their writing and then stick in the picture when they have printed out their work. They may need to work with the formatting commands in the word processor to ensure that there is enough space, perhaps increasing the font size so that the writing and picture both take up the same amount of space.

 *This text occupies the same space as the picture*

Incident in the playground

Display ideas

Enlarge photocopiable page 112 showing the empty thought bubbles and display the children's writing, on the photocopiable sheets and on the A4 sheets, around it.

Other aspects of the English PoS covered

Reading – 2c.

Reference to photocopiable sheet

Photocopiable page 112 provides a picture of an incident in a playground with blank thought bubbles for the children to write in.

WRITING FROM NOTES

To demonstrate an understanding of drafting.
✝✝ *Whole class or group, working as individuals.*
🕑 *At least one hour.*

Key background information

This activity is designed to encourage children to make notes of key points and then use them in their writing. The writing could take the form of a factual account or a fictional story.

Preparation

Prepare your own story which you will read to the children. Alternatively, you might use a news bulletin such as *Newsround* which has been taped the previous day (provided your school or LEA has an Educational Recording Agency licence). Make copies of photocopiable page 113, one for each child. Write down appropriate key words on paper or card for the support activity.

Resources needed

Story or news bulletin (see 'Preparation'), photocopiable page 113, dictionaries, chalkboard, A4 paper, pens, pencils. An example of shorthand for the extension activity. A5 paper/card for the support activity.

What to do

Give out copies of photocopiable page 113 which demonstrates how information can be written in note form. Ask the children when this is useful and why we often rewrite our notes. Ask the children to use the notes on the photocopiable sheet as the basis for a piece of prose. Emphasise the need to make use of all of the information and ask them to elaborate and make the work interesting for the reader.

Tell the children that they are going to have a go at making their own notes. Explain to them that you are going to tell them a story and that they are going to write down key points so that they will remember as much as possible. Explain that they may write while you read or talk and that they will have a few minutes afterwards to add to their notes. Tell them that they should have a go at unfamiliar spellings and that they should not interrupt the story to ask for help.

When the story has been read, ask the children to compare notes. This may be done as a class, or in pairs or small groups. Now ask the children to rewrite their notes in prose. Before they begin, they could check their spellings using a dictionary, or there could be a list on the board of the words which they need most frequently, arising out of the sharing and comparing of their notes.

Suggestion(s) for extension

The children may be interested to see an example of shorthand. Discuss with them ways in which long words might be abbreviated and explain that what is important is that they can read what they have written and understand it.

Some children could be asked to devise their own abbreviations and use these to make notes on a short passage of writing.

Suggestion(s) for support
Children who find the activity difficult could be given some of the key words on pieces of card or paper to help them with their writing from notes.

Assessment opportunities
Look for examples of children appreciating the characteristics of different kinds of writing. Note their abilities to plan and develop their work and to check for errors.

Opportunities for IT
You could make up a short set of notes using a word processor and ask the children to reorder and expand the notes into full prose using the 'cut and paste' or 'drag and drop' facilities. Alternatively, children could use their own notes as the basis for writing their stories.

Display ideas
Display the children's finished pieces of writing alongside their earlier notes to show the extent to which first drafts can be improved upon.

Other aspects of the English PoS covered
Reading – 2b.

Reference to photocopiable sheet
Photocopiable page 113 provides an example of information in note form which the children can convert into prose.

Writing from notes	
Thursday, 25th January	
8.00am	Got up
8.15am	Had breakfast
8.45am	Went to school
9.00am	Headteacher said school closed – no heating
9.30am	Arrived home
9.45am	Went sledging
10.45am	Arrived at hospital
11.30am	X-rays taken
1.00pm	Arm put in plaster
2.00pm	Arrived home
2.15pm	Ate lunch with one hand
3.30pm	Watched other children sledging

WRITING A REPORT
To demonstrate an increased awareness of, and ability to use, the features of report writing.
†† *Individuals or pairs.*
🕐 *At least one hour.*

Key background information
For some children, contact with newspapers may be limited to looking at the television page. This activity provides an opportunity to focus attention on other features. The activity should develop children's abilities to consider eye-catching headlines and to make vocabulary choices which will enliven their writing and make it interesting to read. They will also consider ways in which they can make their writing concise and to the point.

Preparation
Cut out reports from newspapers; exclude the headline on some of them. Ensure that there is a range of reports from different newspapers. Take care to pre-read all reports, especially those from national tabloids. The children could be asked to make their own collections of newspaper reports either in the days leading up to the activity or as a preparatory task on the day of the activity. Make one enlarged A3-size copy of photocopiable page 114 and enough A4 copies to give one to each child or one per pair. Prepare a list of appropriate key words for the support activity.

Resources needed

Newspaper reports (see 'Preparation'), photocopiable page 114, A4 paper, pens, pencils.

What to do

Introduction

Show the children a variety of different newspaper reports on items of interest to them. Give each pair of children a selection of the reports and ask them to read them. Talk about the ways in which the reader is attracted to the reports. Ask the children for examples of interesting vocabulary and dramatic headlines. They can then be given some reports without headlines for which they can devise their own.

Show the children the enlarged copy of photocopiable page 114 and explain that they are going to make notes on what they might write for each headline.

Development

Provide the copies for each individual (or one copy per pair) of photocopiable page 114 and, after the children have made initial notes on the photocopiable sheet, ask them to make up reports to go with one of the headlines. Emphasise the need to attract and maintain the reader's attention. While the children are working, draw their attention to the work of other children in the class and discuss again what makes a good report.

Conclusion

Reports should be shared either by being read aloud or by being displayed. A collection of interesting words or phrases could be made about each topic in the way that many newspapers feature weekly extracts from rival journals.

Suggestion(s) for extension

Children could explore newspapers further and compare reports of the same event. The activity might be used as a prelude to the production of a class newspaper. A selection of reports might be sent to the editor of a local newspaper for comments and the editor might be invited to school to discuss his or her job. Some newspaper offices now have education rooms which children may visit to produce their own newspapers.

Suggestion(s) for support

Children who find the activity difficult could be asked to write shorter reports and be provided with key words. They could work closely in pairs to produce a shared report. Alternatively, they could be given part of a report to complete.

Assessment opportunities

Observe organisation of writing and note choice of words. Note, also, the children's abilities to convey meaning. Look at organisation of work and features of layout and presentation.

Opportunities for IT

The children could use specific newspaper software or a desktop publishing package to create a newspaper style layout for their report. They could look at the format of newspaper pages, where narrow columns are used to make reading easier. The children could then experiment with different font styles and other effects to create eye-catching headlines and bylines. Encourage them to look closely at newspapers, noting how few fonts and styles are used to create a consistent style. If children use the right justification command, they should note its effects on short lines where it often leaves large gaps between words.

Display ideas

Reports could be mounted and displayed against a backdrop of newspapers. A class newspaper could be printed and distributed.

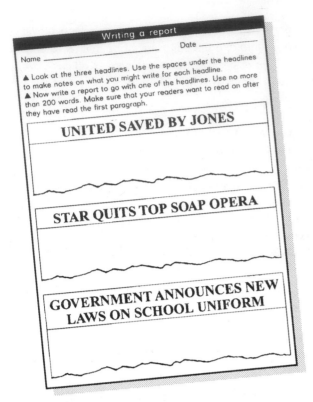

Writing a report

Name _____ Date _____

▲ Look at the three headlines. Use the spaces under the headlines to make notes on what you might write for each headline.
▲ Now write a report to go with one of the headlines. Use no more than 200 words. Make sure that your readers want to read on after they have read the first paragraph.

UNITED SAVED BY JONES

STAR QUITS TOP SOAP OPERA

GOVERNMENT ANNOUNCES NEW LAWS ON SCHOOL UNIFORM

Other aspects of the English PoS covered
Reading – 1b, c; 2c.

Reference to photocopiable sheet
Photocopiable page 114 can be enlarged and used in the introductory part of the main activity as well as being used individually by children, or by children working in pairs, to make notes under each headline before choosing one on which to base their report.

SAYINGS, MORALS AND PROVERBS

To show an appreciation of ways of using planning and drafting to refine and develop writing.
†† *Whole class, working in pairs or as individuals.*
🕐 *At least one hour.*

Key background information
Children often hear, at home or on television, well-known sayings, morals or proverbs. This activity is designed to draw their attention to these and to act as a stimulus for creative, imaginative writing.

Preparation
Talk with the children about what they think different sayings mean. Discuss some of the sayings which parents and other adults use. Show them some examples on the board and ask them to describe situations in which the sayings might

apply. An alternative approach might involve children in collecting sayings at home and bringing them to school for discussion. Make copies of photocopiable page 115 so that you have one for each pair (or individual).

Resources needed
Display of sayings and proverbs, a copy of Aesop's Fables, photocopiable page 115, chalkboard, A4 paper, pens, pencils. Cassette player and blank cassettes for the support activity.

What to do
Begin by talking to the children about the sayings which they know. Read some of Aesop's Fables as examples of stories which have a moral or to which sayings and proverbs could be applied.

Ask the children to provide examples of sayings which they know. This could be done in groups with the children reporting back to the whole class. It may be a good idea to put some incomplete sayings on the board, so that the children can complete these if they do not appear to be familiar with the concept.

Ask the children to work in pairs for a limited time to produce short stories (these may be written in note form) which fit in with sayings which you provide on the board. This may be limited to one saying for the whole class. Let the children share their stories.

Give out copies of photocopiable page 115 and tell the children that they are going to write short stories to go with the sayings. They may do this individually or in pairs. Allow them to begin in note form before developing their stories

Look before you leap

into presentable finished products. It is likely that some of the sayings on the photocopiable sheet will be the same as those previously discussed.

Suggestion(s) for extension

A class assembly could be developed out of the activity with some of the stories being presented to the rest of the school. Children could invent their own sayings and proverbs. They could make a collection of sayings at home by asking parents and other adults for help.

Suggestion(s) for support

Children who find the activity difficult might be asked to work in pairs with more able pupils. The less able could all work on one saying which could be discussed with you, and an oral story might be created by the group, each of whom could then write his or her own story. Those children who experience great difficulty in writing could record their stories on a cassette player or dictate them to you or an adult helper before attempting to write.

Assessment opportunities

Look for evidence of drafting and proofreading. Make a note of the children's abilities to organise stories and select appropriate vocabulary.

Opportunities for IT

The children could use multimedia authoring software to produce an onscreen interactive presentation about each saying. A simple layout would be a front page with an index of sayings, so that if you click on 'A stitch in time saves nine', you are taken to another page where the saying is explained, illustrations added and even the child's own voice added to the presentation, using a microphone and suitable software.

Display ideas

Make a wall display of the collection of sayings made in the extension activity. The children's short stories can be accompanied by display copies of Aesop's Fables.

Other aspects of the English PoS covered

Reading – 2b, c.
Speaking and listening – 1a.

Reference to photocopiable sheet

Photocopiable page 115 provides examples of sayings on which the children can base their stories.

WEATHER WRITING

To produce writing based upon careful observation.

†† *Whole class or group, working individually.*

🕐 *At least one hour.*

Key background information

This activity is designed to develop imaginative writing based on first-hand experience.

Preparation

A period of exceptional weather conditions such as heavy snowfall or drought would be the ideal time in which to undertake this activity. However, it could be attempted in any weather in which it is safe to take the children outdoors. Before this activity it would be a good idea to read poems about the weather to the children.

Resources needed

Weather poems (see above), notebooks (or clipboards and paper), A4 paper, pens, pencils.

What to do

Make sure that the children have notebooks. Take the children outdoors and explain that they are going to walk around quietly without talking to anyone and consider different aspects of the weather. Ask them to look, listen, smell and touch and then jot down brief notes.

When they return to the classroom ask the children to use their notes, and any other ideas that they may have,

and write down ideas as quickly as they can. They could use headings to provide a framework for their ideas such as 'I saw', 'I heard', 'I smelled', 'I felt' and 'I thought'.

When notes have been made invite the children to share some of their ideas with the class before writing them in sentences or lines of poetry on sheets of A4 paper. Encourage the revision of ideas and the addition of new ones. The children could write each idea on a new line, thus leading them towards a poetical format.

Stop the children occasionally to share ideas and problems and to read aloud what has been written.

Suggestion(s) for extension

The children could be shown examples of poems about the weather and could attempt to write their own poetry in a similar style.

Suggestion(s) for support

Encourage the children to list things that they noticed when they were outside, and then to add adjectives to describe them, before being helped to write sentences by an adult helper.

Assessment opportunities

Note the children's abilities to observe carefully and make use of adjectives to enhance their writing.

Display ideas

Display the writing, together with children's artwork or with photographs.

Other aspects of the English PoS covered

Reading – 1d.

SMARTIES

To produce imaginative writing developed through planning and drafting.

†† *Individuals, as part of whole class or as part of a group.*

🕐 *Up to one hour.*

Previous skills/knowledge needed

The children will need to have knowledge of the ways in which authors make use of adjectives and adverbs to enrich their writing.

Key background information

This activity provides a structured drafting process in which children work individually as part of a whole class or group. The teacher dictates the sequencing of events and the pace of the activity demonstrates to children the necessity for note-making.

After the children have finished making notes, ask them to write a poem or a paragraph to describe the Smartie from the first time they looked at it to the time they ate it.

Suggestion(s) for extension
The descriptions could be done in a variety of ways. Children could write an acrostic, a poem or use prose. They could be limited to a maximum of, say, 50 words.

Suggestion(s) for support
Children who find the activity difficult could work in pairs or dictate their ideas to an adult helper. Most children will receive inspiration from being given a second Smartie!

Assessment opportunities
Look at the ways in which the children structure their work. Do they organise their writing to interest the reader? Do they make use of adventurous vocabulary and imaginative expressions?

Display ideas
Ask the children to decorate their work which can then be displayed, together with empty Smartie tubes and packets.

Other aspects of the English PoS covered
Speaking and listening – 1c; 2a.

Reference to photocopiable sheet
Photocopiable page 116 provides instructions for the activity to enable a group of children to work independently when they make notes on each stage of the task.

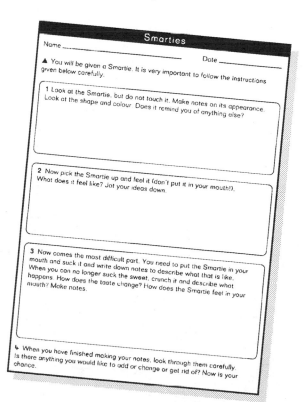

Preparation
Read examples of food writing to the children. These could include Roald Dahl's 'The Centipede's Song' from *James and the Giant Peach* (Puffin, 1995). Encourage the children to describe their favourite and least favourite foods, and write the adjectives and adverbs on the board. Make copies of photocopiable page 116, one for each child.
Note: It is important to ensure that all children may eat a Smartie without side effects. Alternative foodstuffs should be provided in case some children announce allergies.

Resources needed
Examples of food writing (see above), tube of Smarties, photocopiable page 116, scrap paper, A4 paper, pens, pencils, chalkboard.

What to do
Give the children a Smartie each and tell them that they must not touch it, but must look at it carefully. Tell them to jot down their descriptions on scrap paper. They can then use photocopiable page 116; this sheet has questions on it which will help the children to expand their ideas. Emphasise that you are looking for good ideas and that help with spelling will be given later. Encourage them to have a go at words which they are not sure how to spell.

After a few minutes, tell the children that they may pick up the Smartie, but must not eat it. Ask them to describe how the Smartie feels.

Next, tell them that they are going to eat the Smartie, but they must not crunch it until you tell them to. They are to describe sucking the Smartie and then, at the signal, must describe the change in taste when they crunch.

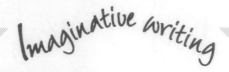

AN INTERVIEW WITH A CELEBRITY

To produce imaginative writing based on research.

†† *Individuals or pairs.*

🕐 *One hour in addition to time spent researching at home.*

Key background information

In this activity the children write an imaginary interview with a celebrity of their choice. They need to do some research to find out about their celebrity and they will be writing in a style which may be unfamiliar to them: reported speech.

Preparation

Tell the children, in advance of the activity, that they may choose any famous person and find out as much as they can about him or her. Show the children examples from magazines and newspapers of interviews with celebrities.

Resources needed

Examples of celebrity interviews from magazines/newspapers, writing materials.

What to do

Read aloud, and ask the children to read, interviews with celebrities. Find examples in which the text is set out as a dialogue without commentary, as well as those which include the comments of the interviewer. The former style may be easier for children to use.

Ask the children to think about the celebrities whom they most admire or in whom they are particularly interested. Then, working individually or in pairs, give them a few minutes to jot down all that they know about the person. Next, ask them to find out more at home by looking at magazines, annuals, newspapers and so on and by talking to adults. Encourage them to make notes from which they can work at school.

When the children have sufficient information, discuss with them again the format of their interview. Most interviews have short questions from the interviewer followed by lengthy replies. Ask the children to include as much information as possible in the celebrities' replies, but to make sure that the text reads as if the celebrity was speaking.

Suggestion(s) for extension

Children might act out the interviews for the class or as part of a class assembly or could tape-record them. The activity could be adapted so that the children research historical figures and write about them. Hot-seating following a class reading session could lead into written accounts of interviews being produced.

Suggestion(s) for support

Children who experience difficulty might be encouraged to compare notes with those children who have found out a lot about a celebrity. They could write in a different form, turning notes into sentences describing the celebrity.

Assessment opportunities

Look for evidence of imaginative use of information and the ability to adopt an appropriate style.

Opportunities for IT

The children could present their interviews using a word processor or desktop publishing package. If a word processor is used, children should be shown how to use the formatting commands to lay out their writing in the form of a dialogue, without positioning text using the space bar. You may also need to set up hanging indents to make sure that the spoken text wraps around in the correct place.

INTERVIEWER	'What do you do when you are not working?'
CELEBRITY	'Well, my favourite pastime is...'

The same effect can be created with a desktop publishing package by setting out two frames and typing directly into them. This method is probably easier for the children to use once the columns have been set up.

INTERVIEWER	'What do you do when you are not working?'
CELEBRITY	'Well, my favourite pastime is...'

Display ideas
Apart from presenting the work in dramatic form, the children's interviews could be featured in a class magazine or newspaper, and displayed in the classroom.

Other aspects of the English PoS covered
Reading – 1c.
Speaking and listening – 1a, b, d.

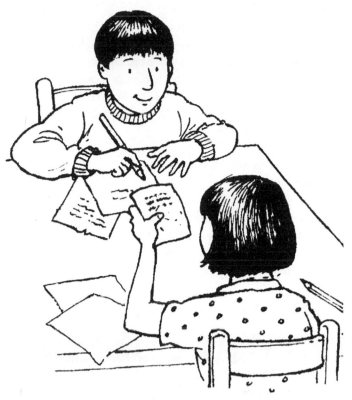

PASSING NOTES

To write for an audience.
†† *Whole class or group, working in pairs.*
🕐 *30 40 minutes.*

Key background information
Most teachers will have encountered an episode of spontaneous note-passing, particularly among older primary schoolchildren. This lesson is designed to channel this into a constructive activity which encourages children to communicate in writing.

Preparation
Before starting the activity, begin the lesson by writing messages to the children on the board or on large sheets of paper so that communication is restricted to writing.

Resources needed
A5 paper/scrap paper, pens, pencils, chalkboard/large sheets of paper, dictionaries.

What to do
Let the children know that they are going to 'talk' to each other without speaking. Ask the children to write messages to each other working in pairs. Tell them that they will be writing to their partner and that they may 'talk' as much as they like, providing they don't speak or use signals. In other words, they may only communicate in writing.

Explain to the children that they may write to each other about any subject and that they will need to make their notes legible and easy to read. They may therefore wish to use dictionaries to help with spellings. Discuss with the children what will be necessary if they are to communicate successfully. Tell the children that they should look at the replies to their notes and see if they made their own questions clear. If replies do not relate to questions, or if the reader responds that he or she does not understand the message, then the author should examine his or her own style.

It may be necessary to remind the children to keep their notes polite, but if the children become restless or overexcited it is probably best to curtail the activity at that point.

Suggestion(s) for extension
Each child could write a note which is not specifically aimed at one member of the class. The notes are then placed in a container and each child draws a note from this and responds to it.

Suggestion(s) for support
Some children may need the help of a partner or scribe to write their messages. The children could work in pairs and send messages to other pairs. However, given that the communication is supposed to be silent, the pairs may have to work away from the rest of the class.

Assessment opportunities
Look for examples of successful communication. Note the extent to which the children are able to elicit responses to their messages through posing clearly structured questions.

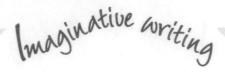

Opportunities for IT

If the school has access to electronic mail through the Internet, the children can write to some unknown children in another school. Show them how e-mail notes are composed: brief but to the point. They could even try adding or making up some emoticons to denote simple emotions (rotate the page 90 degrees to see the full effect). Some common ones are:

- :-) a smiley face;
- :-(a sad face;
- ;-) a winking face to denote humour.

Display ideas

Your messages to the class could be displayed alongside the children's notes to each other.

Other aspects of the English PoS covered

Reading – 1b.

A PLANNED STORY

To demonstrate an awareness of the features and importance of the opening paragraph of a story.

†† *Whole class or group, working individually or in pairs.*

🕐 *At least one hour.*

Previous skills/knowledge needed

Children need to be familiar with the basic conventions of simple storytelling. It would be helpful if they had some experience of telling stories of their own and listening to a storyteller.

Preparation

Before the activity write a short opening to a story yourself. This will enable you to contribute to the class discussion as a fellow-writer. Keep a copy of the drafts of your story opening and annotate each draft, noting carefully the changes you made. Think about some of the key terms you may wish to introduce to the children. These terms might include 'author', 'introduction', 'development', 'focus', 'narrative tension', 'narrative voice', 'suspense', 'plot', 'character'. Collect a selection of children's stories which strike you as having particularly interesting opening paragraphs.

Resources needed

Overhead projector and transparencies of the annotated drafts of your story opening (or the various drafts written on large sheets of paper). Copies of some of your favourite stories written for children, especially ones which have good opening paragraphs (see above). A4 paper, A3 paper, pens, pencils, scissors, glue. Cassette recorder and blank cassette tapes for support activity.

What to do

Give out a sheet of A4 paper to each child. Ask the children to pick up their pencils, close their eyes and concentrate. Invite them to imagine that they are watching a video of their past. When they reach a part of the 'film' which particularly interests them, they are to 'slow' the video down and then 'freeze' the picture at one special 'frame'. Ask them to concentrate really hard on the 'picture' they have 'frozen'. Put the following questions to them:

- ▲ Where are you at this moment?
- ▲ Why are you there?
- ▲ What are you looking at?
- ▲ Who is with you?
- ▲ How are you feeling?
- ▲ What are you thinking?
- ▲ What will happen next?

The children must write down their answers in no more than three words, and only open their eyes to write each answer (the purpose of this is to make sure that they concentrate exclusively on recording their responses as vividly as possible, rather than worrying at this stage about presentation).

When all the children have finished their last answer, ask them to read through what they have written. Show them your own first response and explain why you chose the words you did. Invite one or two of the children to share their work with the whole class in the same way.

Next, the children need to expand each of their phrases into complete sentences. For example, if a child has written 'on the floor' as one of the notes, he or she should now expand the statement so that it might read: 'I was sitting on the floor.' There should be seven sentences in total.

Read your selection of opening paragraphs from children's

stories to the class. Ask the children to tell you whether or not the paragraphs sounded sufficiently interesting to make them want you to read on. This is the stage in the activity where you might want to introduce some of the technical terms outlined in 'Preparation'. Use the discussion time to consider the question: 'What makes an exciting beginning to a story?' Emphasise the fact that no writer ever produces a perfect first draft – not even a teacher!

Tell the children to cut their seven sentences into strips and, taking account of the points raised in the discussion, reorganise them on the page so that they make the most effective opening possible. When the children are satisfied with the sequence they have established, they can paste their sentences in that order on to a sheet of A3 paper. Tell them to number each sentence, and then to write a brief commentary for each one, explaining why they put it in that particular position in the opening paragraph of their story.

Suggestion(s) for extension

Children could make two copies of their story openings and invite a 'response partner' to arrange the seven sentences, just as in the main activity. The two versions could then be compared, with each child arguing the case for his or her particular choice.

A group of four children could pool their 28 sentences and be asked to create an opening paragraph out of seven sentences, and the concluding paragraph to the same story out of another seven. The children may find that they can fit their collective statements into a particular genre, so you could introduce the concept of genre by telling the children that the story could suggest, say, humour, or suspense or mystery.

Suggestion(s) for support

The seven sentence story openings could be recorded on tape. The children could be encouraged to record their different sentence sequences using a variety of tones of voice – angry, happy, quiet, loud and so on – in order to think about the ways in which intonation can influence meaning.

You could let the children do the sequencing exercise in the main activity, substituting seven cartoon-strip pictures for the seven sentences.

Assessment opportunities

Consider, particularly, the reasons the children give you for placing their seven sentences in the chosen sequence. These will help you gain an impression of how well they are beginning to grasp the concept of narrative structure. The most interesting aspects of the activity, as far as assessment is concerned, are the commentaries written on the sheets of A3 and the discussions which ensue in the extension activities. It might be useful to record parts of these so that you can analyse them in some detail.

Opportunities for IT

The children could use a word processor to help them organise and present their seven sentences by moving text around the screen. They could highlight different sections of text in different fonts or colours.

Display ideas

The children's sentences and commentaries on the A3 sheets could make an interesting wall display. You could also write everybody's opening and/or closing line on one

sheet of A3 and display that. The children could design a route map, entitled 'Beginning the Story-writing Journey', and paste their seven sentences as 'milestones' along the route, starting at 'The Beginning' and ending with 'To be continued'.

Other aspects of the English PoS covered
Speaking and Listening – 3b.
Reading – 3.

GROUP WRITING USING PICTURES

To produce co-operative writing based upon drafting, revising and editing.
†† *Whole class in pairs and groups.*
🕐 *At least one hour. The activity may be done over two days.*

Key background information
This activity is intended to foster co-operative writing and encourage drafting and editing, drawing upon the ideas of several children.

Preparation
Cut out colour pictures from colour supplements and magazines, looking for interesting scenes. Do not include any words on the pictures. If you wish to keep the pictures for future use, mount them on card and cover them with self-adhesive plastic film. Use Blu-Tack to stick the pictures on to large pieces of paper. A3 size is ideal, but there should be enough space around the edge of the paper for the children to write.

Resources needed
Pictures mounted on A3 paper (see 'Preparation'), writing materials.

What to do
Explain to the children that they are going to produce a piece of writing which describes a picture, but that they are not going to do so alone. Instead there will be at least six children to help. Each pair will be given a picture stuck to a large piece of paper, and everyone will have a chance to write as much as he or she wishes around the edge of the picture, in order to describe what can be seen, what feelings the picture arouses and what it would be like to be in the picture.

After a few minutes ask the children to pass the pictures on to another pair who should read what has been written and then add their own new ideas. It is important at this stage to stress that they should not point out spelling errors or ridicule others' efforts. The pictures are then passed on

once more for additional ideas from another pair.

Finally, the pictures and the writing are returned to the pair who first had them and the children should be asked to read all of the descriptions before selecting the ideas which they would most like to use in a piece of prose or poetry. They should be encouraged to see that they are the editors and they may decide not to use pieces which they do not feel would fit in well with their writing. They may modify and elaborate upon the notes and they may add new ideas.

Suggestion(s) for extension
The pieces of writing may be done in a variety of different ways. For example, children could be asked to write no more than, say, 50 words or they may be asked to write in blank verse or in rhyming couplets.

Suggestion(s) for support
The nature of the task lends itself to co-operative working which should enable those who encounter difficulties to have the support of more able partners.

Assessment opportunities
Note the children's abilities to revise and redraft the work and their abilities to present a neat, correct and clear final copy.

Display ideas
The final pieces of writing may be displayed with numbers given to each, and the pictures could be displayed on an adjacent board with letters. When children have some free time or when they have completed an activity, they could be

given the task of matching the writing to the pictures, that is, 1A, 2B and so on. If children are told in advance that this is what will happen, it may provide an incentive for them to write accurate descriptions.

Other aspects of the English PoS covered
Speaking and listening – 3b.
Reading – 2c.

THE MYSTERY WALLET

To write in response to a stimulus and to create and describe a character.
†† *Whole class, working individually or in pairs.*
🕐 *At least one hour.*

Key background information
This activity is intended to promote imaginative writing by providing a novel stimulus, which takes the form of a visual aid that the children may refer to as necessary as they work on their writing.

Preparation
Prepare a wallet with various items. These might include a passport-sized photograph, a note and tickets for trains, buses, concerts and so on.

Resources needed
Wallet and contents, writing materials, small pieces of card, chalkboard. Drawing materials for support activity.

What to do
Show the children the wallet. You may wish to add verisimilitude by telling them that it has been handed in at school and that you have to try to identify the owner.

Go through the items in the wallet, perhaps asking the children to take turns to take an item from the wallet. Display the contents of the wallet and write the names of the items on card to label the display. This will help children with spellings when they come to do the writing.

Ask the children what sort of person might own the wallet. Write some of their ideas on the board, but leave sufficient scope for the children to use individual ideas. Tell the children that they are going to build up a picture in words of the owner by examining the wallet's contents. Tell them that this is what detectives would do if they were presented with a limited amount of evidence.

Suggestion(s) for extension
The children might go on to use their descriptions of the owner of the wallet as the basis for stories. Additional items may be introduced such as a suspicious note to encourage imaginative ideas.

Suggestion(s) for support
The activity could be done in pairs. Children who experience difficulty with writing might produce a framework for their descriptions in consultation with you. They could also draw a picture of the owner of the wallet.

Assessment opportunities
Note examples of children revising and redrafting their work and of good use of a narrative style.

Opportunities for IT
Some children could be given a word-processed file containing a list of the items in the wallet and use it as the basis for writing a description of the wallet's owner. They would need to be able to 'cut and paste' or 'drag and drop' text in order to organise the items into groups (for example, credit cards) and put the resulting sentences into the most appropriate order.

The children could also use an art or drawing package to create their own pictures of the owner of the wallet which could be added to their word-processed description. They could also use more specialised face-making software such as *Facemaker* or *SmArt* to draw a face.

Display ideas
Display the wallet and its contents and surround these with pieces of writing. The pictures of the wallet's owner drawn in the support activity could be displayed too.

Other aspects of the English PoS covered
Speaking and listening – 1a.

WHAT HAPPENED NEXT?

To produce imaginative writing developed through planning and drafting.

†† *Whole class or group, working individually or in pairs.*

🕐 *At least one hour.*

Key background information

Some readers may remember the television drama *Dixon of Dock Green*. At the end of each episode the kindly Sergeant Dixon would stand under the blue lamp of the police station and tell us what became of the main protagonists in the story. In this activity the children are asked to decide what became of a character or a number of characters from a story which they have read or had read to them. Ideally, the activity could take place just after you have finished reading a story to the class.

Preparation

Provide a list of the main characters in the story and any other vocabulary which might be useful to the children in their writing. Make copies of photocopiable page 117, one for each child for the main activity and one for each pair for the support activity.

Resources needed

A list of the main characters in your chosen story, a vocabulary list, photocopiable page 117, pens, pencils, scrap paper. Cassette player and blank cassettes for the support activity.

What to do

After completing a story with the children ask them what they think might happen to the characters in the future. Ask them to think of what child characters might do as adults, and discuss what they think deserves to happen to different people in the future.

Encourage the children to make notes on scrap paper before they begin to write in more detail. The writing could take different forms: children might write a story which acts as a sequel to the original or they might be asked to go forward a number of years and describe the life of a character.

Photocopiable page 117 provides a snapshot of the possible future life of a well-known fictional character: Cinderella. After the children have read this sheet, ask them to write a few paragraphs describing a short period of time in the future life of a character in the story of *Cinderella*. The children could give *their* version of what became of Cinderella, or they could write about the future lives of the ugly sisters.

Encourage the children to be imaginative in their choice of lives for their character and reassure them that they have licence to do whatever they wish with the character. A discussion of possibilities might be helpful.

Suggestion(s) for extension

Children could write to authors and send copies of their writing for the authors' opinions. It would be interesting to see the responses they receive.

Suggestion(s) for support

Some children could work in pairs, sharing the writing for mutual support. First they could tape-record their ideas and submit the tape to you so that you could provide key words for the children to use as a framework for their writing.

Assessment opportunities

Look for signs that the children are planning, drafting and revising their work to produce a well-presented final piece.

Display ideas

The children could draw pictures of their characters as they were in the story and as they might be in the future, and these could be displayed, together with their writing and copies of the books.

Other aspects of the English PoS covered

Speaking and listening – 1c.
Reading – 2b.

What happened next?

Cinderella sat gazing out of the window watching the droplets of rain slide down the pane like tears on the cheek of an unhappy child. She felt sad. Life would never be quite the same without her sisters.

The funeral had been a simple one with only a handful of mourners. The sisters had had few friends. This was not surprising, since they had spent most of their lives ordering people around and being unpleasant.

Now that Cinderella was twenty-five, she was able to look back on her life with her sisters. Everyone had called them ugly and it was true that they had not been very attractive. They had treated Cinderella badly and had made her do all the housework, but so had the prince whom she had married. In fact, he had sacked all of the servants as soon as they had returned from their honeymoon.

From dawn until dusk all she ever seemed to do was clean and tidy the palace, look after their two children, and wash Prince Charming's smelly socks. He was dreadfully untidy and he never did a thing to help her. He spent every day with his friends hunting, shooting or fishing. Well, she had had enough. He hardly spent any time with the children and he could not change a nappy to save his life.

Prince Charming was anything but charming. 'Prince Useless would have been a better name for him,' thought Cinderella. He never thought about anyone but himself and he was no more fun to live with than her sisters had been. At least they had grown kinder as they grew older. They used to bring presents for the children, Henry and Elizabeth, and they apologised several times for treating their younger sister so unkindly in the past.

That night, Cinderella planned to have a serious talk with her husband. She had decided to take a job and she had no intention of coming home each night to do the housework. He would either have to employ a housekeeper and a nanny or he would have to stay at home and cook, clean and look after the children himself.

Reference to photocopiable sheet

Photocopiable page 117 provides an example of writing about a well-known character, which can be used as a stimulus for writing about future events occurring in a character's life. (Use the synopsis of *Cinderella* on page 118, if necessary.)

▣ DICE STORIES

To write in response to a stimulus and to develop awareness of a variety of outcomes for a story.

†† *Pairs.*

🕐 *One hour.*

Key background information

Many children may have read 'Fighting Fantasy' stories in which the reader determines the course of the story using dice. You may have read Luke Rhinehart's *The Dice Man* (HarperCollins, 1995) in which the central character decides upon all actions by rolling a die. This activity offers children the opportunity to introduce an element of uncertainty into their stories through the use of a dice to determine content. This should focus attention on planning and drafting.

Preparation

Find a copy of *The Dice Man* and read it or look at 'Fighting Fantasy' books (all published in Puffin).

Resources needed

Examples of dice stories (see above), dice and shakers, writing materials, chalkboard.

What to do

Talk with the children about the 'Fighting Fantasy' stories and explain the format for those who are not familiar with it. Tell them about the idea behind *The Dice Man*. The central character writes down six alternative actions and then rolls a die to determine which he will take. Ask them if they would like to decide their actions by throwing a die. What problems would this present? Which courses of action would they always avoid? (It may be worth pointing out to the children that although many people use the word 'dice' when referring to the singular and the plural the correct term for the singular is 'die'.)

Use the board to write down alternative places in which a story can take place. Let the children offer six different central characters for the story. A good deal of oral work may be appropriate at this stage to familiarise the children with the genre.

Provide dice for each pair of children and tell them that they are going to use the dice to help them to decide the course of events in a story. They could be limited to, say, six throws of the die to determine the story structure and a framework could be produced which the children could use as a plan for their stories. (The work can be done individually if you wish.)

As the children begin to put their stories together, share ideas by reading work aloud and by discussing different approaches to the task.

Suggestion(s) for extension

Children could produce dice stories for others to read, offering alternative paragraphs for the reader.

Suggestion(s) for support

Children who find it difficult to get started on the stories might be helped to devise their alternatives. A small group could brainstorm together, with an adult if possible.

Assessment opportunities

Note the children's abilities to write imaginatively and to organise and structure their writing.

Opportunities for IT

The theme could be used as the basis for a class project using multimedia authoring software to create an interactive 'dice story'. A starting screen could present children with six pictures of the dice numbers. If they throw their own dice and it turns up a three, they click on three and are taken to the relevant location which is described in the text, possibly with the addition of a picture. Again the screen contains six dice numbers and the child clicks on the corresponding number they have thrown to be introduced to the first character and so on.

This is quite a sophisticated structure where each child or pair of children could write a relevant section. You would therefore need six locations, six characters, six events and so on. If different pairs were not shown the writing of the other pairs, they could read the final version without knowing what to expect.

Display ideas

The stories could be put into books and displayed with dice of various sizes made by the children, the dice being used as stands or book-ends.

Other aspects of the English PoS covered

Reading – 2c, d.

ANOTHER WORLD

To produce imaginative writing developed through planning and drafting.

†† *Whole class or group, working independently.*

🕐 *At least one hour.*

Previous skills/knowledge needed

The children need to have read examples of children's literature in which the central characters enter other worlds. They need to think about the different devices which the authors use to take the characters from one world to another.

Key background information

This activity is designed to promote imaginative writing. Many children's stories involve characters being transported from one world to another. Authors use various devices to achieve this. C. S. Lewis has Lucy go through the back of a wardrobe in *The Lion, the Witch and the Wardrobe*. Tom enters an old lady's dream of her childhood when he hears a grandfather clock strike 13 in *Tom's Midnight Garden* by Phillippa Pearce.

Preparation

Find examples of books with other worlds in them. The following may help:
The Lion, the Witch and the Wardrobe and other *Narnia* books by C.S. Lewis (HarperCollins, 1994)
Tom's Midnight Garden by Philippa Pearce (Puffin, 1993)
Alice's Adventures in Wonderland (Puffin, 1994) and *Through the Looking Glass* by Lewis Carroll (Puffin, 1994)
The Secret Garden by Frances Hodgson Burnett (Ravette, 1992)
Marianne Dreams by Catherine Storr (Lutt, 1989)

Resources needed

Examples of books which feature other worlds (see above), writing materials. Cassette player and blank cassettes for support activity.

What to do

Talk with the children about other worlds and what they would like to find in them. Encourage them to make a list of the features which they would include. Ask them to think of ways in which the other world might be entered. Discuss the ways in which this is achieved in some published books. Make it clear that the stories which they are going to write will be displayed and read by their classmates as well as by you.

When they have sufficient notes ask them to write part of a story or a complete story in which characters move from this world to another. Encourage them to plan their work and draft it. Discuss and provide a selection of words which may prove useful. For example:

secret	adventure	entrance	peculiar
magical	unusual	explore	different

It is a good idea to stop the children occasionally, so that ideas can be shared and so that inspiration can be given to those who are finding the task difficult.

Suggestion(s) for extension
Some children may wish to extend their stories into booklets which could be included in a class library. They could go on to write advertisements for their booklets on the lines of those published in newspapers and magazines.

Suggestion(s) for support
Some children may need to devise a framework for their stories in conjunction with an adult or another child. Those who find it difficult to write could use a cassette player and dictate stories on to a tape initially.

Assessment opportunities
Note the children's abilities to plan and draft their work and their use of imaginative narrative.

Opportunities for IT
The children could use an art package to design a cover for a story. The titles could be added using the text facilities.

Display ideas
Display the booklets and advertisements that the children have made in the extension activity.

Other aspects of the English PoS covered
Reading – 1c, d.

FAIRIES AT THE BOTTOM OF THE GARDEN

To show an awareness of writing for the needs of a particular range of readers, using appropriate vocabulary and style.

†† *Whole class or group, working individually or in pairs.*

🕓 *At least one hour.*

Key background information
This activity is designed to promote creative and imaginative writing. A starting point could be the photographs of the Cottingley Fairies. The children are asked to think about what it would be like to meet one of the mythical beings which feature in so many stories written for younger readers.

Preparation
Arrange with a teacher of a younger class that your pupils will be able to share their stories with the younger ones.

Resources needed
Stories which feature elves, fairies, gnomes, dwarfs and so on. Pictures of the Cottingley Fairies if these can be found. Writing and drawing materials.

What to do
Discuss with the children stories which they have read or heard in which mythical beings such as fairies, dwarfs, goblins and elves met people from the real world. Ask them about the characters and whether they were good or bad.

Invite the children to imagine that they were to meet one of the creatures in familiar surroundings, perhaps in their home or garden. Ask them to make notes to answer the following questions:
▲ Where would the first meeting take place?
▲ What would their initial reaction be?
▲ Would they befriend the creature?
▲ Would they be able to keep the creature's existence a secret?
▲ Would they be able to talk to each other?
▲ Can they describe an adventure with the creature?

Tell the children that you would like them to write their stories for younger children and that they will be able to read them with a younger class if the stories are successful. They should be encouraged to consider their audience and give careful thought to the language and vocabulary which they use. The stories can then be produced as small booklets with accompanying illustrations.

Suggestion(s) for extension
Children who feel confident enough to do so could read their stories aloud to groups of children or to whole classes.

Suggestion(s) for support
Some children may need help with structuring a framework for their stories. This could be achieved by writing the questions posed in the 'What to do' section as headings and then brainstorming with a group of children until ideas have been recorded under each heading.

Assessment opportunities
Look for signs that children are drafting and revising their work and are able to use appropriate language and presentational devices for a younger audience.

Opportunities for IT
The children could use a word processor, desktop publishing package or specialised story-maker package such as *Bookmaker* to present their fairy stories. You could design an initial page layout and save it as a template for the children to use. Pictures could be taken from collections of clip art which feature different fairy-story characters. Older or more

able children could set up page numbers, or simple headers or footers including the page number and the title of the book. The stories could then be collated into booklets.

The children could also use multimedia authoring software to create a simple story, complete with sound effects, which the reader can control by clicking on different forwards and backwards arrows.

Display ideas
The illustrated booklets could be covered with self-adhesive plastic film and placed in a library to which younger children have access.

Other aspects of the English PoS covered
Speaking and listening – 1a, b.
Reading – 1d; 2a.

CAUTIONARY TALES
To show an appreciation of range of genre and an ability to produce imaginative, drafted writing.
†† *Individuals or pairs.*
⏱ *One hour.*

Key background information
Hilaire Belloc's cautionary verses may be used as a stimulus for this activity. Children are encouraged to produce imaginative writing which relates to aspects of health and safety.

Preparation
Read examples of Belloc's verses to the children: 'Jim', 'Matilda' and 'Rebecca' are usually well received.

Resources needed
Selected Cautionary Verses by Hilaire Belloc (Puffin, 1987), scrap paper, A4 paper, pens, pencils, chalkboard.

What to do
Talk with the children about the verses and ask them to think about other aspects of health and safety which might provide themes for cautionary verses. List their ideas on the board and ensure that some key spellings are included with the list.

Tell the children that they are going to write their own cautionary tales. They do not have to be in verse and they could be written in prose. Encourage them to spend time jotting down their ideas on scrap paper and emphasise that they do not have to make use of all of their notes, but that they may select from them the ideas which they wish to use and leave out the others.

When the children have spent time making notes, ask them to organise these into a framework for a story. This

might involve listing events in the order that they will be written about. When the children have done this ask them to begin to write their stories in sentences.

As the children work, try to spend time with individuals, helping them with organisation and with editorial points. When the children have produced a draft version of their stories, provide good quality paper for them to write them out carefully. The results may be read aloud.

Suggestion(s) for extension
Some children could attempt to write in verse or rewrite their stories in verse.

Suggestion(s) for support
Children may need to work out a framework for the story with an adult. Encourage the use of 'magic lines' when children are unsure of spellings and cannot get help easily. This method involves children writing as much of a word as they can and drawing a line for the rest, and then continuing their writing until someone can help them.

Assessment opportunities
Note the children's abilities to make successful use of drafting techniques in order to develop their imaginative writing.

Display ideas
The cautionary tales which the children have written in the activity could be displayed in the classroom alongside copies

of Hilaire Belloc's *Selected Cautionary Verses*. The stories could be taped and listened to during reading sessions.

Other aspects of the English PoS covered
Reading – 1d.
Speaking and listening – 1a.

MINI SAGAS

To demonstrate an ability to edit and revise writing to make it more concise.

†† *Whole class or group, working individually or in pairs.*

🕐 *One hour.*

Key background information
In this activity children have to write a piece of prose with an exact, pre-defined number of words. The objective is to encourage them to consider carefully their choices of vocabulary and to develop drafting and editing skills.

Preparation
Photocopy the examples of mini sagas on photocopiable page 118. You will need one copy for each child (and one per pair for the support activity).

Resources needed
Photocopiable page 118, scrap paper, A4 paper, pens, pencils.

What to do
Talk with the children about the mini sagas on the photocopiable sheet and discuss the ways in which stories have been told using a limited number of words. Ask them what the author has done to achieve this and discuss the ways in which unnecessary words can be left out.

Tell the children that they are going to write a mini saga of exactly 50 words. They must draft their work and revise it so that they stick to the word limit. Some children may wish to make up their own stories, while others might use stories they have already written or stories which are well known to them.

The children will experience most difficulties when they try to limit themselves to exactly 50 words. Encourage them to look very closely at the words they have used and to look for opportunities to eliminate words. This is a useful opportunity to discuss the use of a word such as 'got' which is usually unnecessary. For example, 'I have got a new coat' would read equally well as 'I have a new coat'.

Encourage the children to look at each other's writing to advise on ways of sticking to the word limit. When the children have finished read pieces aloud.

Suggestion(s) for extension

The children could go on to try different word limits, making use of appropriate textbooks and attempting to précis paragraphs.

Suggestion(s) for support

Pairs of children could be presented with two or three simple sentences and be asked to condense them into one.

Assessment opportunities

Look for appropriate vocabulary use and note the children's abilities to write concisely.

Opportunities for IT

An original story could be provided for the children in the form of a word-processed file, which the children can load into a word processor and redraft to make a shorter version. The children should be shown how to use the word processor's word count so that they can check that they have written only 50 words.

Display ideas

Make a wall display of copies of the mini sagas and invite readers to look for places where words could be eliminated.

Other aspects of the English PoS covered

Reading – 2b, c.

Reference to photocopiable sheet

Photocopiable page 118 provides examples of mini sagas and suggestions for titles for mini sagas that the children can write themselves.

NURSERY STORIES FOR YOUNGER CHILDREN

To demonstrate an awareness of writing for a particular audience, using appropriate vocabulary and style.

†† *Individuals or pairs.*

🕐 *Two hours.*

Key background information

In this activity children are asked to write a story for younger children in their school which may be based upon a traditional story or may be their own invention.

Preparation

Read examples of nursery stories to children and discuss the language the authors have used. In order to establish that traditional stories can be interpreted in interesting and amusing ways, read Roald Dahl's *Revolting Rhymes* (Puffin, 1984) and other revised versions of traditional tales.

Resources needed

Nursery stories, Roald Dahl's *Revolting Rhymes*, A4 paper, pens, pencils, dictionaries.

What to do

After discussing nursery stories with the children, explain that they are going to write stories for younger children and ask them how their writing might have to be presented if the children are to enjoy the stories. Older children tend to feel rather more confident about their writing when they are told that they might have to make it simpler for a younger audience.

Ask the children to think carefully about the story they are to write and to draw up a plan and list the words which they are likely to need for each section. Where the vocabulary might be too complex for younger children, encourage them to use dictionaries to find alternatives.

When the stories have been completed they can then be presented to the younger children. The children could use a serial form for the presentations of their stories.

Encourage children to rehearse reading their stories before they present them to the younger children.

Suggestion(s) for extension

The stories could be illustrated and made into a book which could be added to the library of the younger children's classroom. Younger children could tell the older ones stories which the older children could then write for them in an appropriate style.

Suggestion(s) for support

Some children might feel insecure about presenting stories to younger children, some of whom may be more able. In such cases children should work in pairs to write and present the stories. Some rehearsal will be particularly important here.

Assessment opportunities

Note appropriate choices of vocabulary and evidence of careful presentation which takes into account the needs of the audience.

Opportunities for IT

The books could be written using a word processor or desktop publishing package. If a desktop publishing package is used, the children can easily make new frames for pictures or position the text on the screen.

The children could also use multimedia authoring software to create their nursery stories, which the reader can control by clicking on different pictures to move forwards and backwards. They could use a microphone linked to the computer to record sound effects or their own voices reading the story.

Display ideas

The books for the younger children could be displayed in their classroom.

Other aspects of the English PoS covered

Speaking and listening – 1b.

HOROSCOPES

To show an ability to write in an extended range of genre.

†† *Whole class, working individually and in groups.*

🕐 *One hour.*

Key background information

This activity is intended to develop children's abilities to write in different styles and may be used as part of the production of a class newspaper.

Preparation

Collect examples of horoscopes, making sure that you have enough for all the months.

Resources needed

Examples of horoscopes, list of star signs, writing materials.

What to do

Ask the children if they know which birth signs they were 'born under'. If they do not know show them a list and let them find out. Explain that some people look at their horoscopes and believe that astrologers can predict their futures by looking at the stars. It is worth pointing out that many people are very sceptical about this too!

Having discussed the nature of horoscopes with the children, ask them to think of the sorts of things which they could predict would be likely to happen. The activity might

be done during a week in which probability was being studied in mathematics.

Read examples from magazines and newspapers so that children are aware of the style in which horoscopes are written. Ask them to try writing a prediction for one star sign and let them share these to exchange ideas. When they feel confident about continuing let the children work in groups, dividing the star signs between them to produce a forecast.

Stop the children occasionally to share ideas and to provide examples for those who are experiencing difficulties.

Suggestion(s) for extension
Children could make collections of horoscopes from newspapers and magazines and look for common themes and predictions.

Suggestion(s) for support
Children who find the activity difficult could work in pairs. Some children may not be familiar with horoscopes and may need to see plenty of examples.

Assessment opportunities
Note the children's abilities to write in an appropriate style and make use of appropriate vocabulary.

Opportunities for IT
Children could write and edit their horoscopes using a word processor. As the text entry is quite short, attention could be focused on redrafting at the keyboard. The resulting horoscopes could be added to a class newspaper.

An interactive horoscope could be created using multimedia authoring software. A title page could show each of the signs of the zodiac, so that when the child clicks on their sign another page opens up showing the horoscope written by the class. It could even include a link to a page

giving more information such as the birthstone and characteristics of people born under that sign.

Display ideas
The work could be included in a class newspaper or a class book. A display of signs of the zodiac and an explanation of the origins of each could accompany a wall display.

Other aspects of the English PoS covered
Reading – 3.

IF I WERE A...

To write in response to a particular stimulus.
†† *Whole class or group, working individually.*
🕐 *One hour.*

Key background information
This activity is designed to encourage children to use information about animals as the basis for a piece of imaginative writing.

Preparation
The activity may be done as part of topic work on living things. Children will need to be familiar with the characteristics of certain animals and will require access to reference sources. Read examples of literature which is written from animals' points of view, for example *Black Beauty* by Anna Sewell (Puffin, 1994), and *Watership Down* by Richard Adams (Penguin, 1993).

Resources needed
Reference books (including encyclopaedias and texts on animal life), fiction books which are written from the standpoint of the animals themselves (see above), writing materials. Cassette player and blank cassettes for support activity.

What to do
Ask the children to choose animals which they would like to find out more about. Ensure that they have adequate access to reference sources and encourage them to make notes. Ask them to share the knowledge they have acquired and explain that they are going to write a short piece as if they were the animal they have researched. They could describe what it would be like to be able to fly, or run very quickly or climb with great agility. They might consider what they would miss if they were not human and what effect humans would have upon them.

If they find it difficult to write in the role of an animal, read more examples from children's literature and discuss them with the children. Read the children's work aloud to provide further examples.

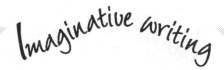

Suggestion(s) for extension

The children could build up a data bank which included the characteristics of different animals. They might be given headings for their research including: size, habitat, diet, life expectancy, predators and unusual features.

Suggestion(s) for support

Children could work with partners or could record their ideas on tape. They could be provided with a series of partially completed sentences to help them to write about their chosen animal. For example:

> I am a _____ .
> I live in a _____ .
> I eat _____ and _____ .

Assessment opportunities

Look for consistency in writing in the first person and for examples of well-written, imaginative writing.

Opportunities for IT

Children could also use the information they have collected to make a branching database. This differs from the traditional database in that the children teach it about new animals through a series of questions. As the questions must yield a 'yes/no' answer this makes it an excellent language activity. Once the database has been built, children can use it like a key, so the dialogue with the computer might be:

> Is it an animal?
> *answer yes would lead to*   Does it live on land?
> *answer no would give*   It is a whale.

Display ideas

A display of photographs and pictures of animals drawn by the children could accompany a display of the children's writing.

Other aspects of the English PoS covered

Reading – 2c.

A MILLION POUNDS

To show an ability to produce imaginative, speculative writing.

†† *Whole class or group, working individually.*

🕐 *One hour.*

Key background information

In this activity the children are asked to think about what it might be like to acquire a great deal of money. Children show a great interest in the National Lottery, even though they need to be 16 before they can buy tickets. Some may own Premium Bonds, however, and the top prize for these is one million pounds. This activity is intended to promote imaginative writing and not to encourage gambling, so it may be worthwhile spending some time discussing some of the problems which gambling can cause.

As an alternative to mentioning gambling in any form, children could be asked to imagine that they had acquired the money because they had written a successful song, or a story which had been made into a film. They might receive the money in return for selling the patent for a wonderful invention. Alternatively, they might find a valuable painting in the loft or be given a reward for saving a multimillionaire's life.

Preparation

If possible, find examples from newspapers of stories about people becoming wealthy. Make copies of photocopiable page 119, one copy for each child.

Resources needed

Photocopiable page 119, writing materials. Newspaper cuttings for the extension activity (see above).

What to do

Talk to the children about money and ask them to think about whether winning a lot of money would actually make them any happier. Talk about how the money might be used to make other people's lives easier. Ask the children to imagine what it would be like to find themselves suddenly very

wealthy. Tell them to work individually and to make brief notes on the sort of things they would do with the money. Photocopiable page 119 provides a framework for making notes.

When the children have made notes, ask them to write them in prose, revising and editing as they do so. As they work, ask individual children to read out extracts to the class.

Suggestion(s) for extension

Children could use newspaper cuttings to research stories about people who have acquired large amounts of money. They could discuss whether they think that these people have been fortunate to have gained this money. They could write their own feature on a real or imaginary wealthy person.

They could also write about the precise moment when a person realised that he or she was very wealthy. As a prelude to this, discuss some of the vocabulary which might be useful for writing about such an occasion: 'lucky', 'fortunate', 'excited', 'ecstatic', 'surprised' and so on.

Suggestion(s) for support

Children who find the activity difficult could make lists of what they would do with their money. They might be provided with a bank of words following a brainstorming session with you.

Assessment opportunities

Look for evidence of drafting and editing to produce interesting, imaginative writing.

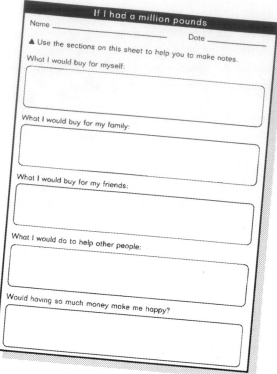

Display ideas

The newspaper cuttings about prize winners, or people who acquire wealth suddenly, could be displayed, together with the children's work.

Other aspects of the English PoS covered

Speaking and listening – 2a, b.

Reference to photocopiable sheet

Photocopiable page 119 provides a pro forma for the children's note-making about acquiring a million pounds.

MR MEN STORIES

To demonstrate greater understanding of writing for a range of audiences and improvement in presentational skills.

†† *Whole class or group, working individually or in pairs.*

🕐 *At least one hour. The activity may be spread over several days.*

Key background information

This activity provides an opportunity to encourage children to write for a real audience using a familiar format. Since the stories are to be illustrated, Mr Men make an ideal theme as they can be drawn quickly and easily.

Preparation

Make sure that all the children are familiar with Roger Hargreaves' *Mr Men* stories (World International Publications). Provide a display of the different Mr Men and read some of the stories to the children.

40

Resources needed

Mr Men books, pictures of Mr Men, writing and drawing materials.

What to do

Introduce the children to some of the Mr Men by showing them pictures and reading the stories. Tell them that they are going to create their own Mr Men and ask for ideas for what they might be called. It may be a good idea to provide a lengthy list of adjectives which could describe personality traits as an aid for the children.

Explain that the stories are to be written for a younger audience and tell the children that they will need to consider the vocabulary which they use carefully.

Ask the children to draw their Mr Men, encouraging them to keep pictures simple and in the Hargreaves style. This should enable even those with limited artistic abilities to produce something presentable, and it should mean that the pictures are easily reproducible. When the drawings are finished the children may go on to produce cartoon-strip stories for their characters. Encourage the production of simple storyboards before they go on to make final copies.

Encourage children to show each other their stories at regular intervals in order to provide examples and maintain interest in the task.

Suggestion(s) for extension

Some children could go on to produce their own Mr Men books which could be read to younger children in serial form.

Suggestion(s) for support

Children who experience difficulty could be presented with limited text which they could add to and then draw accompanying pictures. They could also tell their stories to an adult helper who could help to develop the story by asking questions about it.

Assessment opportunities

Note the children's abilities to write in an appropriate style for their audience.

Opportunities for IT

The children can use an art or drawing program to create their Mr Men pictures using simple drawing techniques. They will need to know how to create shapes and lines, alter their size, change the colour and so on. Children could design their basic Mr Man character and then save it so that it may be used at a later date as the basis for another picture. The pictures could be included in a version of the story using a word processor or desktop publishing package.

Display ideas

The stories could be presented as cartoon strips or as small books in the Hargreaves style.

Other aspects of the English PoS covered

Reading – 1a, c.
Speaking and listening – 1a.

ADJECTIVE, NOUN, VERB POEMS

To demonstrate an ability to use adjectives, nouns and verbs in poetic writing.
†† *Whole class.*
⏱ *50–60 minutes.*

Key background information

This activity is intended to provide children with the beginnings of a metalanguage which they can use to help them to discuss their work. It also provides an opportunity to develop their ability to write imaginatively.

The children will need to be introduced to, or reminded of, the concepts of adjectives, nouns and verbs. Many people avoid using the terms, preferring instead to talk about

describing words, naming words and doing words. However, it is helpful for children to know terms which can be useful when they are discussing their reading and writing. It is no more difficult to learn that the name for a doing word is a verb than it is to learn in mathematics that a shape with four equal sides and four right angles is called a square.

It should be noted that the same word may sometimes act as a different part of speech. For example, 'fast' could be an adjective in 'fast car', an adverb in 'run fast', a verb in 'fast for a day', and a noun in 'hold a sponsored fast'.

The writing created in the activity will take the form of elementary poetry, but will allow scope for children to expand this into more complex structures.

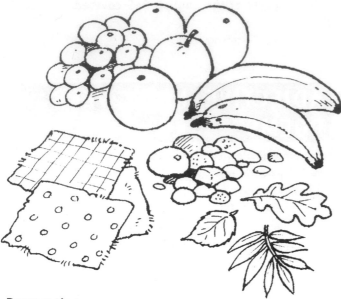

neighbour who will add adjectives. The papers may then be passed on again or passed back for verbs to be added. The paper could be set out as in the following example:

ADJECTIVE	NOUN	VERB
slow	train	moves
long	journey	ends
brown	leaf	falls

This activity may subsequently be tried independently, with the focus being narrowed so that it is based upon a single theme. Alternatively, children may work together in pairs.

Suggestion(s) for extension
Encourage the children to expand the clauses into sentences and produce more elaborate poems or pieces of prose. The children could be asked to write stories in which each sentence contained a noun, a verb and at least one adjective. They may go on to include adverbs in their writing. (See the activity 'Use of adjectives' on page 88.) It is important that children see that words can have different functions and that a word may sometimes be used as a different part of speech and may not always be, for instance, a noun. The following words could be discussed in different contexts:

green	A green shirt
	Eating your greens
fool	She is a fool.
	It is easy to fool him.
run	I can run quickly.
	He scored a run at cricket.
top	It was snowing at the top of the mountain.
	It was the top song in the charts.
	He could not top his best performance.

Suggestion(s) for support
Provide words on cards to help those who find the activity difficult. A game could be introduced with sets of equal numbers of adjectives, nouns and verbs with children taking turns to choose words to produce adjective-noun-verb sequences.

Assessment opportunities
Look for evidence of experimentation with vocabulary and for appropriate use and understanding of the parts of speech.

Display ideas
The poems or pieces of prose written in the extension activity could be displayed, together with the items used to provide stimuli for words used adjectivally. Appropriate word cards can be placed around the display.

Other aspects of the English PoS covered
Speaking and listening – 3b.

Preparation
Compile lists of adjectives, nouns and verbs. For the support activity make individual word cards, each card with a word which can be used as a noun, adjective or verb written on it. (Provide equal numbers of nouns, adjectives and verbs.) Collect objects which can be used to evoke words which are interesting adjectives. These could be items which may be found in the classroom or they may be things which the children could taste, smell or touch such as fruit, leaves, pieces of cloth or stone.

Resources needed
Items which can be connected to adjectives when being described (see above), A5 paper, chalkboard, pens, pencils. A4 paper for extension activity. Card, felt-tipped pens for support activity.

What to do
Begin the lesson by writing a list of nouns on the board. Choose words which are relevant to a topic the children are studying or to something which they can see. Talk about the words and ask what kind of words they are. If no one is able to describe them, tell the children that they are called nouns. Ask the children to provide more examples of nouns. You may add to the list or produce a new list as they do so.

Next ask the children to provide words which describe each of the nouns and write these on the board in front of the nouns. Tell them that these words are called adjectives. It would be useful to make use of visual aids (as mentioned in 'Preparation') to provide stimuli for interesting adjectives.

Now ask the children to say what each item might do. For example, if they had 'bright light' they might add that it 'glows'. Elicit from them or tell them that these words are called verbs.

Ask each child to make a list of six nouns on a small piece of paper with one word underneath another. When they have done so ask them to pass their list on to a

GREETINGS CARDS

To use the features of rhyming poetry to write for a real audience.

†† *Whole class or group, working as individuals or pairs.*

🕒 *One hour for writing in addition to time spent designing cards.*

Key background information
In this activity children produce rhymes for greetings cards. The activity should develop their phonic knowledge and their ability to use rhyme.

Preparation
Make a collection of greetings cards which have verses inside them. Often the verses are rather simplistic and the rhymes contrived.

Resources needed
Greetings cards, chalkboard, scrap paper, card, pens, pencils, art materials.

What to do
Give out some commercially made greetings cards and ask the children if they think the message is more effective when written in verse than in prose.

Introduce the activity and explain that the children are going to make greetings cards for people whom they know.

These may be birthday cards, get well soon cards, Christmas cards, or congratulations cards of various kinds. Before they begin the writing activity the children could design their cards in draft form on scrap paper and then complete them when they have produced their verses.

Talk to the children about the examples of rhymes on the cards and ask for suggestions for pairs of words which rhyme. List these on the board. Explain the features of verse such as the use of capital letters at the beginning of each line. Initially, children may find it easier to work on rhyming couplets, but may go on to look at other features of rhyming poems such as rhyming alternate lines.

Ask the children to experiment in draft form with rhymes and encourage them to discuss these with their neighbours. Read examples aloud.

When the children seem confident about writing verses help them to draft and revise their work before they write final copies into cards.

Suggestion(s) for extension
Those children who are particularly successful at writing verse might be encouraged to retell a story which they had previously written or read in rhyme.

Suggestion(s) for support
Children who experience difficulty might be encouraged to work with an adult helper to produce a list of useful rhymes which could be used at the end of each couplet and which they could use in their writing.

Assessment opportunities
Note the children's abilities to use appropriate rather than contrived vocabulary. Look for evidence of drafting and the ability to prepare a neat, correct and clear final copy.

Opportunities for IT
The children could create their verses for the greetings cards using a word processor. They might look at a range of different cards and see the sorts of fonts used and then select one which they feel is appropriate for their card.

The children could also use an art or drawing package to design a picture for the front of the card. The text and pictures could be combined using a word processor, desktop publishing package or drawing software to make the greetings cards.

Display ideas
It is important that the cards are sent to people if children are to feel that they have written for a real audience. However, copies of the verses could be displayed alongside commercial examples.

Other aspects of the English PoS covered
Reading – 1c.

WRITING

LIMERICKS

To show an awareness of and ability to use poetic structure and rhyme.

†† *Whole class or group, working individually or in pairs.*

⏱ *45 minutes.*

Key background information

This activity should help children to think about rhyme and should encourage them to experiment with vocabulary use. Limericks have five lines in which the final words of lines one, two and five rhyme and the final words of lines three and four rhyme. Lines one, two and five each have eight or nine syllables, while lines three and four have five, six or seven each. An example would be:

There was a young student from Hull,
Who found life incredibly dull.
All things curricular,
And Maths in particular,
Pounded away in her skull.

Preparation

Find examples of limericks to read to the children. *The Children's Book of Comic Verse* edited by Christopher Logue (Piccolo, 1980) is a useful source. Prepare a list of rhyming words to have in reserve for the children to use in their limericks. Make copies of photocopiable page 120, one for each child or pair.

Resources needed

Examples of limericks (see above), a list of rhyming words, photocopiable page 120, chalkboard, writing materials.

What to do

Read some limericks to the children and show them one or two on the board. Ask them to look at the rhyme scheme and work out what it is. It may be worth providing a few limericks which do not have a final line and asking the children to suggest possible endings. Give out copies of photocopiable page 120. This sheet provides examples of limericks which are incomplete. Ask the children to fill in their own words in the spaces provided. It should be emphasised to them that there is no one correct way of completing the limericks but they must continue the rhyme scheme and their limericks must scan in the right way.

Tell the children that they are going to make up their own limericks, but first they will need to work out some collections of rhyming words. You may provide some to start them off, but encourage them to work in pairs to find their own. Once the children have a stock of words ask them to try writing limericks. Remind them that the last words of the first two lines rhyme with the final word of the fifth line and the last words of the third and fourth lines rhyme with each other.

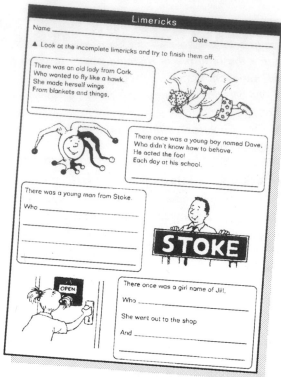

It will probably be necessary to stop the children regularly to remind them of the format and to share examples of good work.

Suggestion(s) for extension

Groups of children who have been successful in the activity might work together in fives, taking turns to write a line each for five limericks and passing them around for completion.

Suggestion(s) for support

Some children could be given rhyming words for the ends of each line of the limerick and be asked to complete them. Note, too, their knowledge of sound–symbol correspondence.

Assessment opportunities

Note children's abilities to follow the format of a limerick and to make use of rhymes.

Opportunities for IT

The children could write their limericks using a word processor. An alternative approach would be to give them a word-processor file containing the start of a limerick. They could load it into the word processor and complete it. A similar approach would be to use a complete limerick and ask the children to change highlighted words to create a new limerick on the same theme. These activities would encourage children to explore the structure of the limerick while developing editing and drafting word-processor skills.

Display ideas

Display the children's work, together with published limericks and an explanation of the limerick form. Also display some

incomplete limericks, perhaps offering small prizes for the best efforts at completing them.

Other aspects of the English PoS covered
Reading – 1b, c.

Reference to photocopiable sheet
Photocopiable page 120 provides incomplete limericks for the children to complete.

REWRITING LYRICS FOR HYMNS

To demonstrate an increased awareness of the poetic form.

†† *Whole class or small groups, working in pairs.*

🕐 *One hour.*

Key background information
This may be a suitable activity as a preparation for a class assembly. Children can be encouraged to look closely at the words of common hymns and to devise their own lyrics which are appropriate for the theme of their assembly. The activity also provides an opportunity for teachers to discuss some of the more complex hymn lyrics with the children. Another purpose of the activity is to encourage children to understand the concept of scanning and metre.

Preparation
Provide examples of three hymns which are popular with the children.

Resources needed
Examples of hymns, dictionaries, scrap paper, A3 paper, pens, pencils, overhead projector (optional).

What to do
Talk to the children about their forthcoming assembly and tell them that they are going to write the words for the hymns themselves so that they will fit in with the theme for the assembly. Encourage them to think about the way in which the words fit the tunes.

It may be best to begin by having the children sing some hymns and discuss the lyrics and the ways in which they fit the tune.

This activity is probably best done in pairs with children choosing hymn tunes and then working together to ensure that their lyrics scan. Ask them to try out the lyrics by singing them to the established tune.

Encourage the children to try one verse at a time and to present the verses to you or their classmates as they are completed so that they may be revised and redrafted in the light of responses.

When children have successfully completed a verse ask them to write the words on a large piece of paper or on an overhead projection sheet so that the rest of the class can attempt to sing them.

Suggestion(s) for extension
Children could study the lyrics to well-known hymns and carols and use dictionaries to find out the meaning of some of the more difficult words and phrases. They could go on to produce 'translations' and could read these to the class. 'Hark the Herald Angels Sing' may be a good starting point at Christmas time and 'When a Knight Won his Spurs' at other times.

Suggestion(s) for support
Children who encounter difficulties should work with small groups or more able partners. They could be given partially completed verses after you have discussed the verses with them and be asked to complete these.

Assessment opportunities
Note examples of children successfully producing lyrics which scan, rhyme (where appropriate) and which include appropriate vocabulary.

Opportunities for IT
You could prepare a word-processed file containing the lyrics of the hymn to be altered. The children could then work as a group, using a word processor, to create a new hymn.

Display ideas
The individual hymn sheets could be made into a class hymn book and put on display.

Other aspects of the English PoS covered
Reading – 1d; 3.

their audience will include younger children and adults and that they will have to use appropriate language so that everyone can understand the prayers. Many prayers involve responses or repetitions from the congregation. The children might be encouraged to include such prayers which foster audience participation.

Discuss with the children the vocabulary which is commonly used in prayers and make a collection of words which appear frequently, such as 'amen', 'beseech', 'thy', 'thee', 'divine' and 'thine'. The children might be encouraged to consider alternative vocabulary which may be more meaningful to their audience. Explain that they will be reading the prayers and encourage them to practise this.

Suggestion(s) for extension
Children could be encouraged to look at prayers used in a range of religions and to note similarities and differences. For example, they could study and make notes on the different terms for God, the different style of prayers, the ways in which prayers are ended, and the things for which the gods are petitioned and thanked.

Suggestion(s) for support
Children who experience difficulty in writing could dictate their prayers to a scribe.

Assessment opportunities
Look for evidence of appropriate use of vocabulary and style.

Display ideas
A class prayer book could be produced, with presentational devices such as illuminated first letters and illustrations included.

Other aspects of the English PoS covered
Reading – 2c.
Speaking and listening – 1a; 3a.

PRAYERS

To show a greater understanding of range of genre.
Individuals or pairs.
30–40 minutes.

Key background information
When children perform class assemblies they are sometimes asked to make up prayers. This activity encourages them to consider the content of their prayers and the appropriate styles which they might use.

Preparation
Read examples of prayers from different religions as well as from Christian prayer books.

Resources needed
Prayer books, examples of prayers used at school, writing materials.

What to do
Discuss prayer with the children and ask them about why people pray. It may be a good idea to emphasise that many prayers do not ask for things for the person praying, but ask for things for others or offer thanks.

Explain to the children that there will be prayers at their forthcoming assembly and that you would like them to write them. Talk about the examples of prayers which you have found and ask the children if they know any more. Children from non-Christian faiths should be involved if possible.

Ask the children to consider the theme for the assembly and to think about appropriate prayers. Remind them that

HAIKU

To use a well-defined poetic structure.
Whole class or group, working as individuals.
30–40 minutes.

Previous skills/knowledge needed
For this activity the children will need to understand what a syllable is. The activity might follow work in music in which children clap their names syllable by syllable.

Key background information
The activity should develop children's knowledge of syllables as well as their abilities to draft and revise work to fit in with a rigid format.

Preparation

Find or write examples of haiku to show to the children, and photocopy page 121 so that you have one copy for each child.

Resources needed

Examples of haiku, photocopiable page 121, chalkboard, writing materials.

What to do

Revise work on syllables. Clap names and ask the children to identify them. Try clapping names of television programmes or football teams too. Remember, there may be several correct answers. Next, ask the children to make up sentences with given numbers of syllables. They might write the sentences to describe a friend, or a favourite team or programme.

Explain that a haiku is a Japanese poem which has three lines and consists of seventeen syllables altogether. The first line has five syllables, the second has seven and the third five. Haiku are intended to make a simple statement or describe something in a very concise way. Read examples to the children and show them examples on the board. Then give out copies of photocopiable page 121.

Tell the children that they are going to write their own haiku. You might ask them to stick to one theme or you may let them choose their own subjects. Encourage them to draft their work and to try to think carefully about the words that they use so that their poems have exactly the right number of syllables. Share the children's ideas with the whole class throughout the activity and at the end.

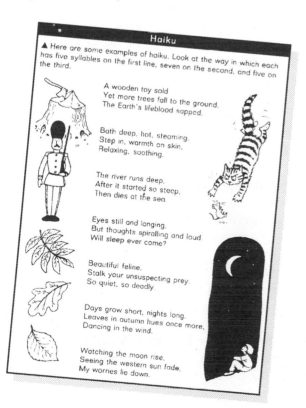

Suggestion(s) for extension

Some children may go on to write other poems with restricted formats. An example would be a cinquain which has five lines of two, four, six, eight and two syllables respectively.

Suggestion(s) for support

Ask the children to write their ideas down in brief note form. They can then be helped to produce a haiku which conforms to the syllable pattern. Discussion with you about vocabulary and the nature of syllables will be important at this stage.

Assessment opportunities

Make a note of the children's use of the drafting process and their abilities to reflect upon their choice of vocabulary.

Opportunities for IT

The children could use a word processor to write their haiku poems. If there is a speech facility they could listen to their poems to check that each line has the correct number of syllables.

Display ideas

Display the finished work under a heading 'Haiku'. In order to give depth to the display these short poems can be mounted and then stuck to matchbox-sized packets before being pinned to the wall.

Other aspects of the English PoS covered

Reading – 1c, d.

Reference to photocopiable sheet

Photocopiable page 121 provides examples of haiku which the children can read before writing their own.

NOVEMBER

To write poetry within a structured scheme.

†† *Whole class or group, working individually or in pairs.*

⏱ *40–50 minutes.*

Key background information

Hood's poem 'No!' is structured so that each line begins with 'No' and comprises a statement about things which are lacking in November. The final line is simply 'November!'. In this activity the children are asked to follow the same format to write their own poems about November. For obvious reasons, the activity is best done in November!

Preparation

Read 'No!' by Thomas Hood to the children. This poem can be found in *The Puffin Book of Classic Verse* edited by Raymond Wilson (Viking, 1995).

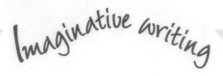
Resources needed
Poem 'No!' (see above), chalkboard, dictionaries, writing materials.

What to do
Read the poem 'No' and discuss its format with the children. Ask them about the things which November makes them think about and make a note of their ideas on the board.

Explain that they are going to write their own 'No!' poems, using a similar format to that used by Thomas Hood. Ask them to work with a partner to jot down ideas and begin to draft and compose their poems. It may be a good idea to remind them that their work need not rhyme. Encourage children to use their dictionaries to help them to find suitable words.

As the children work, ask them to read aloud examples of lines which they are particularly pleased with.

Suggestion(s) for extension
Children might produce similar poems using the same format but a different beginning. For example, a 'yes' poem could be about 'yesterday', an 'un-' poem might be about 'united', or a 'for' poem might be 'forever'.

Suggestion(s) for support
Children who find the activity difficult might work with an adult helper to produce a group poem.

Assessment opportunities
Note evidence of appropriate vocabulary choices and the ability to draft and revise work.

Display ideas
Display the children's work, together with Hood's poem. The children could present their poems in an assembly during the month of November.

Other aspects of the English PoS covered
Reading – 1d.
Speaking and listening – 1a.

 IF...

To write imaginatively in a structured form.
†† *Whole class or group, working individually.*
🕐 *At least one hour.*

Key background information
This activity is based upon Rudyard Kipling's poem 'If'. The children are asked to produce their own versions of the poem after considering all the qualities which they feel an adult should possess.

The activity should allow you to assess children's abilities to use the characteristics of a different form of writing and to write imaginatively.

Preparation
Find a copy of Rudyard Kipling's 'If'. One of the books in which the poem may be found is *Classic Poems to Read Aloud* (Kingfisher, 1995). Write the poem out or word-process it and make an enlarged copy of it on a sheet of A3 paper.

Resources needed
Kipling's poem (see above), writing materials, chalkboard.

What to do
Talk with the children about adulthood and ask them what they think are the main characteristics of being an adult. Some of their ideas might be written on the board, or they could use a piece of paper to make their own notes.

Kipling's poem deals with being a man, but it might just as easily refer to adulthood in general. This should be stressed to the children. Read the poem to the children and ask them for their opinions. Then ask the children to work independently to write their own poems about adulthood using Kipling's style. Let the children refer to your copy of 'If' written on the large sheet of paper when working on their own versions. Emphasise that when they write their poems they should not copy Kipling's work, but should use its structure.

Suggestion(s) for extension
Some children might wish to attempt a different style of poem after writing the 'If' poem. This could involve using a different word, such as 'when', to begin each line or it might involve them in creating their own style.

Suggestion(s) for support
For children who find the activity difficult ask them to choose a selection of appropriate words. These could then be written down for them to use in their own poem.

Assessment opportunities
Note children's abilities to make appropriate vocabulary choices, to plan and draft their work and to adopt a suitable style.

Display ideas
The large sheet with Kipling's poem on it could form the centre piece for a display of the children's work.

Other aspects of the English PoS covered
Speaking and listening – 1a, b, c; 2a; 3b.
Reading – 1a, c, d.

Non-fiction writing

The activities in this section are designed to develop a range of written styles. Many of the tasks involve children in writing in formats other than prose, including reports, explanations, notes, letters and diaries.

The programmes of study set out a variety of different forms of writing which children should be taught to use. The activities in this chapter are designed to provide opportunities for children to explore these forms of writing in response to a wide range of stimuli.

Some of the activities are related to children's literature, while others involve examining the styles used in diaries, recipe books, postcards and questionnaires. The activities are intended to afford children the opportunities to write as real writers in response to the types of stimuli which real writers experience.

Many of the activities demand the use of forms of layout other than prose. It is important that children see that they are writing in these different styles for a purpose and that their writing is to be read by others.

WRITING

TELEGRAM NOTES

To use notes as a starting point for writing in prose.

♦♦ *Whole class or group, working individually or in pairs.*

🕐 *45 minutes.*

Key background information
This activity should help children to organise writing around key words, making use of adjectives, verbs and adverbs to enhance their writing.

Preparation
Make use of photocopiable page 122 (you will need one copy for each child or pair) and examples of your own to show children how telegrams were set out.

Resources needed
Examples of telegrams, photocopiable page 122, chalkboard, writing materials.

What to do
Show the children examples of abbreviated writing with only key words provided. The examples on the photocopiable sheet can be used as a starting point. Talk about telegrams and the way in which they were written to minimise the use of words to save costs. Although telegrams are no longer used, children may have seen them in old films or on

children's educational programmes such as *How we used to live.*

Ask the children to take one example and help you to rewrite it in sentences. This may be done on the board. Encourage them to think of ways of embellishing the writing to make it more interesting to the reader.

When the children seem confident about the work, provide them with more examples to work on individually or in pairs. Stop the children occasionally to share their ideas with the rest of the group.

Suggestion(s) for extension
The activity may be reversed, with children being given passages of prose to reduce to telegram form. The passages may be prepared by you or could be taken from novels or textbooks.

Suggestion(s) for support
Talk through the telegram message with the children and ask them to tell you orally about it. Provide key words which will help them to produce writing independently.

Assessment opportunities
Note the children's abilities to write in sentences and to make use of punctuation marks correctly. Look for examples of appropriate choices of vocabulary.

Opportunities for IT
Children could use a word processor to compose their telegram in the shortest number of words possible. They should be shown how to use the word-count facility.

Display ideas

Display abbreviated writing and expanded writing on adjacent boards and ask children to match the pieces.

Other aspects of the English PoS covered

Speaking and listening – 3b.

Reference to photocopiable sheet

Photocopiable page 122 provides three examples of messages in a telegram style which the children can rewrite in prose.

DID YOU KNOW THAT?

To record information concisely and accurately.

†† *Individuals or pairs.*

🕐 *10–15 minutes.*

Key background information

In this activity children take turns to be responsible for a class 'Did You Know?' board by looking for interesting facts in reference books and recording these in brief on card for display.

Preparation

Make a 'Did You Know?' board and cut pieces of card (on which each fact can be written). Make a slot on the board which will hold the current fact of the day. Photocopy page 123, one copy for each child or one per pair.

Resources needed

Danny, the Champion of the World by Roald Dahl (Puffin, 1994), 'Did You Know?' board (see above), photocopiable page 123, reference books, card, paper, pens, pencils. Drawing materials for extension activity.

What to do

Read chapter 12 of *Danny, the Champion of the World* to the children. In this chapter Danny considers what he would put on the stone tablet above the door of his school. Talk about the interesting facts which he suggests could be written there each day, and ask the children if they would like to do something similar.

Explain that they can create their own bank of interesting facts and that these can appear on a special board each day or each week. Tell them that they will need to take turns to find interesting facts and that they may find these at home, in reference books or in the local library. Any facts must be verified by checking in an encyclopaedia or reference source.

Show the children how they can record the facts in an interesting and carefully presented way. They may work in pairs, with a rota being drawn up to show when children will be responsible for the 'Did You Know?' board.

Suggestion(s) for extension

Children could produce their own booklets of interesting facts and illustrate these.

Suggestion(s) for support

Children who experience difficulty could work with the support of a partner or an adult helper. A selection of simple reference books should be provided for them.

Assessment opportunities

Look for evidence of careful presentation and an ability to write in an appropriate style using correct punctuation.

Opportunities for IT

Children could use a CD-ROM encyclopaedia to search for interesting facts on particular topics. If children work in pairs on this activity, their list could be printed out using a word processor to make a class book.

Display ideas

The 'Did You Know?' board can be placed on the outside of the door to the classroom or in a similarly prominent position so that children can see it every day.

Other aspects of the English PoS covered

Reading – 2c.

Reference to photocopiable sheet

Photocopiable page 123 provides a few examples of interesting facts, together with spaces for the children to add their own.

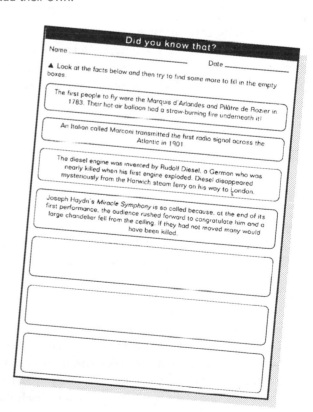

BOOK COVERS

To demonstrate awareness of the importance of layout and presentation and an ability to use some features to present work attractively.

†† *Whole class or group, working individually or in pairs.*

🕐 *One hour.*

Key background information

This activity is designed to encourage children to examine the features of book covers and to replicate these in their own covers for well-known books or, if possible, their own stories.

Preparation

Prepare a collection of books that have covers which include a brief synopsis of the plot, enticing the reader to want to read them.

Resources needed

A selection of appropriate books (see above), paper/card, coloured pencils, felt-tipped pens, pencils.

What to do

Show the children examples of book covers and draw their attention to the publishers' blurbs in which the stories are summarised and made to appear interesting and inviting.

Discuss with the children the styles which are adopted and ask them to think of ways in which they would tell someone briefly about the qualities of a book which they wished to persuade that person to read. Make a note of some of the words which can be used in such persuasive writing so that children may use these for reference.

Ask the children to produce their own book covers for books which they have read. It is probably best to ask them to complete writing in draft form before they embark on lengthy illustration work in case mistakes are made in writing on the cover. The covers could be illustrated using coloured pencils lightly so that writing may be superimposed. It may be a good idea to ask children to produce new covers for books in the class library which have become worn. This will give real purpose to the activity.

As the children work, draw attention to interesting use of vocabulary and emphasise the need to be concise.

Suggestion(s) for extension

Children could write their own books and produce covers for these.

Suggestion(s) for support

Some children could work in pairs to gain ideas from a partner.

Assessment opportunities

Look for evidence of appropriate vocabulary use and the adoption of a suitable persuasive style.

Opportunities for IT

An art or drawing package could be used to create the picture for the front of the cover, or scanned versions of the children's own line drawings could be used. The writing for the cover could be done using a word processor or desktop publishing package. However, the full cover (both text and illustration) would be most easily produced using a desktop publishing package with a landscape-sized page divided into three sections: front cover, spine and back cover. More adventurous designs could also include the flaps as well. For larger books the jacket may have to be put together in parts so that appropriate-sized pages can be printed out.

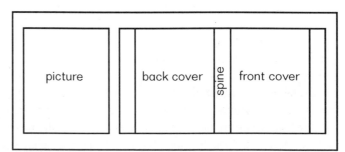

Display ideas

Covers can be used on books in the class library or might be displayed together with the originals.

Other aspects of the English PoS covered

Reading – 2b.

RECIPES

To show understanding of the features of instructional writing and an ability to use these.

†† *Whole class or group, working individually.*

🕐 *One hour in school and work at home with family.*

Key background information
In this activity the children create a class recipe book using information they have found at home. The activity should offer an opportunity for discussion about different styles of writing. Recipes include lists as well as instructions, written either in prose or in a sequence of numbered sentences.

Preparation
Parents and guardians need to be informed about the activity and be asked to help by discussing recipes with the children and helping them to make notes. It is important that parents do not simply write the recipes for the children but that they provide information which children can record in note form.

Resources needed
Examples of recipe books, writing materials.

What to do
Show the children examples of recipes from published books and explain that it is important to provide clear guidance so

that people can use the recipes successfully. Talk about different aspects of recipes including lists of ingredients and directions. Make sure that they have notes on the recipes which they are to write up.

Leave copies of cookery books on each table so that children have a reference point for style and a resource for checking spellings of foodstuffs and culinary terms. Ask the children to use their notes to write out recipes. Encourage them to begin by listing ingredients and to go on to provide step-by-step instructions for preparing the foods. As the children work stop them occasionally to read aloud their recipes and to invite constructive comments from other children.

Suggestion(s) for extension
Some children could edit the recipes, in consultation with the authors, and collate them to produce a class recipe book.

Suggestion(s) for support
You may need to act as a scribe for some children or provide supportive partners. Some children could make lists of ingredients and then list key words for instructions, before being helped to write in sentences. A word bank may be useful.

Assessment opportunities
Look for evidence of appropriate style for recipes, clarity of instructions and the ability to write chronologically. Note the children's abilities to present work carefully.

Opportunities for IT
The children could write their recipes using a word processor. By looking at recipe books they will see how recipes are laid out and usually include lists and illustrations. Show the children how to use formatting commands such as tabs to line up a list of the ingredients.

150g wholemeal flour	50g coconut
100g butter	50g muscovado sugar
50g fine oatmeal	1 egg

The children could then draw appropriate pictures for their recipes, or even add pictures scanned from photographs of the cooked recipes.

Display ideas
The recipes collated in booklets in the extension activity could be displayed and made available for sale to parents at school bazaars and so on.

Other aspects of the English PoS covered
Reading – 1b.

NEW YEAR'S RESOLUTIONS

To write in response to a stimulus.
†† *Whole class, working individually.*
🕐 *One hour.*

Key background information
This activity is intended to allow the children to experience a different style of writing. For obvious reasons, it is best done at the beginning of the year.

Preparation
Write your own list of New Year's resolutions to show to the children.

Resources needed
Example of New Year's resolutions, writing materials. Cassette player and blank cassettes for the support activity.

What to do
Talk with the children about New Year's resolutions and ask if they or their families have made any. Talk about your own resolutions and show the children the style in which they are written.

Explain to the children that you want them to think carefully about some resolutions which they could make and that they will be able to keep a record of their resolutions by writing them down so that they can check on whether they have kept them or not as the year progresses.

Ask the children to begin by making notes rather than writing sentences. A short period of silent working may help

them to get their ideas down quickly. When they have made notes ask them to tell you and the rest of the class some of their ideas and ask them to express these in sentences, orally, before they go on to write them. Since resolutions can be very personal it may be a good idea to tell the children that they may keep some of them private and only present those which they do not mind other people knowing about. The resolutions could be collected in by you and then read aloud anonymously, with children being invited to guess who had written them. Before doing this you might ask if anyone would rather not have his or her resolutions revealed to the class.

The lists of resolutions could be kept and returned to later in the year so that children could decide which of the resolutions they had kept. This might lead to a further piece of writing about the difficulties of keeping resolutions.

Suggestion(s) for extension
Children could make up resolutions which they would like to see other people keep.

Suggestion(s) for support
Some children could record their resolutions on a cassette before writing them with your help or working in pairs with other children.

Assessment opportunities
Look for evidence that children are able to adopt an appropriate style of writing.

Display ideas
Resolutions could be put into a book for occasional reference to see if people had kept their resolutions.

Other aspects of the English PoS covered
Speaking and listening – 2a.

NEIGHBOURS

To use adjectives to improve descriptive writing.
†† *Whole class, working individually.*
🕐 *One hour.*

Key background information
In this activity the children are asked to write about a person whom they know well and to organise their writing into paragraphs, making frequent use of adjectives to describe the characteristics of their subject.

Preparation
Show the children how they can make a character web. Photocopiable page 124 provides an example which you can photocopy for those children who need it.

Neighbours

Tom

- very forgetful
- has lots of friends
- likes sport
- laughs a lot
- kind to animals
- confident
- always losing things
- works hard at school
- gets cross when he loses at football
- generous
- can be aggressive
- loses temper easily

Resources needed

Photocopiable page 124, writing materials, dictionaries, thesauruses, reading books, chalkboard.

What to do

Explain that the children are going to think about people whom they particularly like. Show them the character web on photocopiable page 124 and ask them to make their own, noting the characteristics of their chosen person. Ask the children to think about the person whom they have chosen and to consider their qualities. Discuss the examples and talk about the kinds of words which might be used.

Encourage children to make use of dictionaries, thesauruses and their reading books to gain ideas. Ask them to look at the descriptions of characters in their reading books and see if the author builds up a picture in words.

From time to time, stop the children and ask them to share any adjectives with which they are particularly pleased. Write these on the board so that everyone can see them.

Suggestion(s) for extension

Children could make use of character webs as a starting point for story writing.

Suggestion(s) for support

Provide a list of good and bad characteristics for people and ask children to select from these, as well as adding their own. The list may be developed through a brainstorming session with the children.

Assessment opportunities

Note the children's understanding of the term 'adjective' and their ability to use reference sources.

Display ideas

Display a blank character web around a picture of a well-known personality. Invite the children to write adjectives to describe the celebrity on card and place these around the picture.

Other aspects of the English PoS covered

Reading – 2b, c.

Reference to photocopiable sheet

Photocopiable page 124 provides an example of a character web which the children can use as a model from which to make their own webs.

MY IDEAL ROOM

To use the features of descriptive writing in response to a stimulus.

†† *Whole class or group, working individually.*

⏲ *One hour.*

Key background information

This activity will provide children with the opportunity to write non-fiction on a subject to which they can easily relate, making use of adjectives to enhance their writing.

Preparation

Some of the colour supplements in weekend newspapers include features on celebrities' favourite rooms or on their houses. Other colour magazines have similar features. Make a collection of these.

Resources needed

Photographs of rooms and articles about people's ideal rooms, *Flossie Teacake's Fur Coat* by Hunter Davies (Armada, 1984), writing and drawing materials.

What to do

Show the children examples of 'ideal' rooms and ask them to tell others about the things which they would have in their ideal rooms and about the ways in which they would like them to be decorated. Explain the subjective nature of an article on an ideal room, that is, the fact that one person's ideas about a room which is ideal will not necessarily be the same as another person's. You can then read the descriptions of Bella's room and Flossie's room in *Flossie Teacake's Fur Coat*. Bella's room is extremely untidy, whereas Flossie's is tidy and orderly. This will lead to discussion about the extent to which people's ideal rooms can differ.

Ask the children to draw a floor plan or a picture of their ideal room before they write about it. This should provide a reference point for their writing. It may also be useful to brainstorm with the children to build up a word bank of useful terms.

Tell the children that they are going to write descriptions of their ideal rooms. Encourage them to make the rooms seem attractive and inviting and emphasise the need for adjectives to help them to build up a clear picture in the minds of their readers. Encourage children to read their descriptions aloud and to comment constructively upon each other's efforts.

Suggestion(s) for extension
Children might go on to describe an ideal house. They could include descriptions of gardens and features of the outside of the building.

Suggestion(s) for support
Children could draw large pictures of their ideal rooms and label these rather than using prose.

Assessment opportunities
Look for evidence of careful descriptions and appropriate use of adjectives.

Opportunities for IT
The children could use a drawing package to create a plan of their ideal room. They will need to know how to draw and position and resize lines and geometric shapes to represent furniture. Older children could draw their room to scale, fill the shapes with colour and create a key.

Alternatively, children could use a framework package like *My World 2* (SEMERC) with an appropriate file such as 'T&D Home' or 'Design a 3D Bedroom' to create their ideal room on screen and then print it out.

Display ideas
Display pictures and models of ideal rooms, together with descriptions. If models are made, descriptions could be pinned to the sides of boxes.

Other aspects of the English PoS covered
Speaking and listening – 1a.

PREPARING A TALK TO THE CLASS

To make use of revising and drafting as a starting point for preparing a verbal presentation.

†† *Whole class or group, working individually or in pairs.*

🕐 *One hour in the classroom with additional time at home or spent on research at school.*

Key background information
This activity is designed to present children with a task which involves careful planning and preparation in writing and which will lead to an oral presentation.

Preparation
Find examples of notes which you or a colleague have made prior to teaching a lesson. Make copies of photocopiable page 125, one for each child or one per pair.

Resources needed
Lesson notes, photocopiable page 125, writing materials, reference books.

What to do
Show the children how you prepare for teaching by making notes of key points, and let them know that the notes are useful as an aide-mémoire when you are teaching.

Explain that the children are going to prepare talks for their classmates and that they will need to gather information and then organise it so that they can make their presentations interesting and informative. Some children may wish to work independently, while others may work in pairs.

Set a time-limit for each talk of between five and ten minutes and give the children time to look for information both at school and at home. It may be a good idea to prepare a list of possible topics for the talks, based upon the children's interests. Photocopiable page 125 provides some possible topics as well as a framework for the talks.

Monitor the progress of the children's note-making and encourage them to refine their notes until they have a clear sequence of headings for their talk. Encourage them to make their notes brief and legible, and stress that the notes are written for their benefit rather than for a wider audience. Emphasise that they are not going to read their notes aloud, but will be using them to help them to remember the key points of their talk.

It may be a good idea to allow the children to present their talks over a period of a couple of weeks so that they do not have to listen for lengthy periods and so that those who have completed the task can provide an example for those who have not. Encourage the children to allow time for questions at the end of their talks.

Suggestion(s) for extension
Some of the talks might be presented to other classes or to the rest of the school in assembly.

Suggestion(s) for support
By working in pairs, children should be able to offer mutual support and divide up the research task.

Assessment opportunities
Look for examples of well-organised notes which are structured and provide a sound basis for oral presentation.

Opportunities for IT
The children could use a word processor to create an outline talk, using a series of headings which can then be expanded after researching the topic, with information being restructured. The children's prepared talks could be printed out, perhaps using a larger font style so that the text is easy to read.

Older or more able children could use a multimedia authoring package to create a visual presentation, which could be shown to the class using a large monitor. This could combine different forms of information such as pictures, text and sounds.

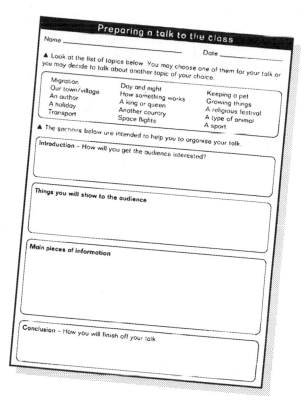

Preparing a talk to the class

Name _____ Date _____

▲ Look at the list of topics below. You may choose one of them for your talk or you may decide to talk about another topic of your choice.

Migration	Day and night	Keeping a pet
Our town/village	How something works	Growing things
An author	A king or queen	A religious festival
A holiday	Another country	A type of animal
Transport	Space flights	A sport

▲ The sections below are intended to help you to organise your talk.

Introduction – How will you get the audience interested?

Things you will show to the audience

Main pieces of information

Conclusion – How you will finish off your talk.

Display ideas
Children's talks could be tape-recorded or filmed on video for presentation to parents and to other classes.

Other aspects of the English PoS covered
Speaking and listening – 1a, b.

Reference to photocopiable sheet
Photocopiable page 125 provides a framework for the talks.

CLASS RULES

To communicate ideas in writing.
†† *Pairs or small groups.*
🕐 *One hour.*

Key background information
This activity is designed to allow children to consider the rules which they think should apply in their classroom and to write these in a clear and concise way in an appropriate style.

Preparation
The activity might arise out of a perceived need on behalf of the teacher or the children for a code of conduct within the classroom. Children could be shown examples of rules for clubs and societies, so that they understand the style of writing which tends to be used.

Resources needed
Examples of rules, writing materials.

What to do

Talk with the children about why we have rules. Ask them which rules they think are good and which they disapprove of. Ask them to work in pairs or in small groups to produce rules for the classroom. Emphasise the need to be very clear about the rules and to make them easy to read, understand and remember.

When appropriate, stop the children and bring them together to discuss the rules which they have devised. A scribe might be appointed to make a note of the rules which most people agree with. Discuss some of the key words which have been used and talk about their spellings.

Ask the children to decide which of the rules are the most important and invite a few children to write these up for further discussion. Ultimately, a set of class rules which can be displayed may be devised.

Suggestion(s) for extension

Children might go on to write rules for games and other activities.

Suggestion(s) for support

Children who experience difficulty should work with more able partners or make use of an adult as a scribe. They might prepare their rules in note form, drawing upon a word bank which could be provided for them.

Assessment opportunities

Note the children's abilities to adopt an appropriate style for the task.

Opportunities for IT

The class rules could be edited using a word processor, with pictures added if appropriate. This could be printed out in a large font suitable for display in the classroom.

Display ideas

Many classroom and schools now display codes of conduct which have been devised in consultation with the teachers.

They act as a reference point for teachers and pupils when behaviour is unacceptable. The class's agreed set of rules could be displayed in a prominent position. The activity might lead to a presentation in assembly.

Other aspects of the English PoS covered

Speaking and listening – 2a, b.

POSTCARDS

To use an appropriate vocabulary and style of writing for a particular audience.
†† *Whole class, working individually.*
🕐 *One hour.*

Key background information

This activity might be used after the summer, Easter or half-term holiday as an alternative to asking children to write about their holidays. The activity requires children to write in a brief and informal way.

Preparation

Bring to school, and ask the children to find from home, a selection of holiday postcards which have been written and posted. Some shops specialise in selling these, and it may be interesting to show the children examples from many years ago.

Resources needed

Postcards, photographs from magazines, card, writing and drawing materials.

What to do

Discuss the postcards with the children and read some examples of what people have written. Talk about the way in which a lot of information can be given concisely, and ask them how they would write the same information if they had more space.

Tell the children that they are going to write a postcard about their recent holiday. There may be many who will not have been away for a holiday, but they could write about a

visit or about what they had done at home. Ideally, there will be a real audience for the writing such as a pen-pal or a friend from another class. Talk about the key pieces of information which they would like to include, and encourage drafting so that children can see how much room they have for their writing and can write at an appropriate length.

Discuss the drafted versions with children, before they go on to produce final copies. For the final versions, the children may wish to make postcards using photographs from magazines, or illustrations which they produce themselves.

Suggestion(s) for extension
Ask the children to write postcards which famous people in history might have written at particular times, for example Napoleon at Waterloo, Guy Fawkes from prison, William or Harold at Hastings.

Suggestion(s) for support
Work with children to produce a list of the things which they wish to write about, and provide them with key words.

Assessment opportunities
Note children's abilities to write concisely and with an economy of words, while still conveying a message.

Opportunities for IT
The children could be given a desktop publishing template for their postcard and allowed to write their message so that it fits into the available space. Children could even design a picture for the other side of the postcard using an art package, or an image taken from a CD-ROM.

Display ideas
Display postcards with photocopies of the messages displayed next to them.

Other aspects of the English PoS covered
Reading – 1c.

 ## FLOW CHARTS

To use the features of layout and presentation of a flow chart.

†† *Whole class or group, working individually or in pairs.*
⏱ *One hour.*

Key background information
Children's writing often takes the form of prose. This activity is intended to encourage them to use another style in which layout and presentation need to be considered carefully. Such presentation may reduce the number of words used, as well as providing an eye-catching and easy-to-understand message to the reader.

Preparation
Make copies of photocopiable page 126, one for each child or pair.

Resources needed
Photocopiable page 126, chalkboard, scrap paper, A3 paper, pens, pencils.

What to do
Give out copies of the flow chart on photocopiable page 126 and ask the children if they agree with the way the process of making tea is described. Draw their attention to the way in which the text is provided briefly and consecutively. Then ask them to complete the photocopiable sheets.

Talk about a familiar activity such as getting ready for school in the morning. Make use of the children's descriptions of what they do to produce a flow chart on the board. Discuss the way in which key information can be provided without the use of sentences and explain that this is another way of recording information.

Tell the children that they are going to produce their own flow charts. It is a good idea to ask for suggestions for subjects and write these on the board so that children may see the sorts of topics they might use.

Encourage children to try out their ideas in draft form and to revise these and check spellings and so on before producing final copies for display. Final copies can then be made on A3-sized paper so that children can talk through their charts with the rest of the class or group.

Suggestion(s) for extension
Children could incorporate flow charts into their work in other areas of the curriculum, for example a flow chart of the life

WRITING

of a historical character, a flow chart of the life cycle of a butterfly, or a chart of a river's progress.

Suggestion(s) for support
The number of stages to be completed in the flow charts could be reduced, and the children could be provided with partially completed charts.

Assessment opportunities
Look for evidence of clear and appropriate presentation.

Opportunities for IT
Although it is possible to purchase specific software for creating flow charts, this activity can also be done using a drawing package. To start children off, you could produce a master flow chart document which has all of the flow chart symbols already created and placed around the edge of the drawing area. The children can then retrieve this file and duplicate or copy the required symbols, moving them into place and adding the appropriate lines, arrows and text.

Display ideas
Display the children's flow charts, together with pictures depicting some of the activities, which have been cut out of magazines.

Other aspects of the English PoS covered
Speaking and listening – 1a, b, c.

Reference to photocopiable sheet
Photocopiable page 126 provides an example of a flow chart which the children can complete.

PROGRAMMES FOR SCHOOL ACTIVITIES

To write for a real audience of parents and visitors to the school.
✦ *Small groups or pairs.*
🕐 *At least one hour.*

Key background information
This activity provides children with an opportunity to develop presentational skills and non-fiction writing for a real audience. They will produce a programme for distribution to visitors at a school event.

Preparation
Provide examples of programmes for plays, concerts and sporting events.

Resources needed
Programmes, card, paper, pens, pencils.

What to do
Show the children the programmes which you have collected, and explain that when people attend an event they like to have some information about the people taking part and about the event itself.

Look at the information which the programmes provide and examine the features of presentation. Discuss the ways in which the programmes have been produced and made to look attractive so that people will buy them.

Discuss a forthcoming event (a class assembly, school play, sports day and so on) and tell the children that they are going to produce programmes for visitors to the school. Explain that it will be very important that their final copies are attractively presented and accurate and that they should try ideas out first before using good quality card or paper.

Children can work in pairs or small groups to produce different sections of the programmes, and the word processor can be used to enhance layout. The final product should be sufficiently well-produced for it to be presentable to visitors. It is worth emphasising this point throughout the activity.

It is important to gain feedback on the quality of the end-product from parents and other visitors when the programmes are sold or given away at the event.

Suggestion(s) for extension
Children might go on to look more closely at the professional production of programmes. Their attention could be drawn to features such as advertisements, prices and the information provided. They might be asked to compare the quality of different programmes and to write a short account expressing their opinions.

Suggestion(s) for support

The division of labour in the production of the programmes should lend itself to participation by everyone, but children who experience difficulties with writing should not be restricted to the role of illustrators. Their ideas can be written down by others, so that they contribute to the text.

Assessment opportunities

Look for evidence of understanding of the importance of careful presentation and note the children's abilities to draft and revise their work.

Opportunities for IT

The children can use a word processor or desktop publishing package to produce the programme. Attention should focus on the organisation of the information in the programme and the possible use of pictures to make it more interesting. Children should be shown how to use formatting commands to lay out the programme, without using the space bar to line up text. Attention should be drawn to design features, particularly readability and the use of bold, underline, italics or font size rather than using a variety of different fonts.

Display ideas

Display the children's programmes, together with a class collection of professionally produced programmes.

Other aspects of the English PoS covered

Reading – 1c.

DIARY OF A DAY

To write in the style of a journal.

👬 *Whole class, working independently.*

🕐 *A series of short periods of writing throughout the day.*

Key background information

Children need to know how diaries are kept. This activity should enable children to consider the different ways in which people make use of diaries and should provide them with an opportunity to write in a style appropriate for a journal.

Preparation

Collect a number of books which provide examples of diary writing. Examples could be read from Samuel Pepys, Anne Frank and even, selectively, Adrian Mole. In this activity the diary entries divide the day up, so examples of diaries which are presented in a similar way would be useful.

Resources needed

Examples of diaries (see above), writing materials. Cassette player and blank cassettes for support activity.

What to do

Discuss diaries with the children and talk about the reasons for keeping them. Explain that some people keep diaries to remind them of what they are going to do, while others write about events which have already happened.

Read and show the diary entries to the children, either at the beginning of the day on which the diary is to be written, or on the day prior to the activity. Explain that they are going to keep a diary of the day. Talk with them about the things which they might include and tell them that they are going to begin by writing about the day so far. Later they will have a number of chances to update their diaries.

Provide opportunities throughout the day for the children to make brief entries in their diaries. This might be done before and after break times and at the end of the day. It may be

appropriate to ask the children to take their diaries home to complete.

On the following day ask the children to read their diaries aloud and compare different versions of the day's events. The varying interpretations may lead to a discussion of newspaper reporting and the recording of historical events.

Suggestion(s) for extension

Children might go on to keep a weekly diary or may produce a diary of the day once a term. The results could be kept in a portfolio with other work so that the children may later look back upon their time in school.

Suggestion(s) for support

Provide key words for children who find the activity difficult. Some children might record their diaries using a cassette player.

Assessment opportunities

Note the children's abilities to write in a diary format and their use of interesting vocabulary.

WRITING

Opportunities for IT

The children could use a word processor to write their diary. Show them how to lay it out with a subheading for the time of each entry. They could use the word processor's features to add the time and date automatically.

Display ideas

A display headed 'Diary of a Day' could be mounted and examples of famous diaries could be displayed alongside it.

Other aspects of the English PoS covered

Reading – 1c, d.
Speaking and listening – 1a.

BOOK REVIEWS

To write questions related to the reading of books.

†† *Individuals.*

🕐 *Ongoing activity.*

Key background information

Children's book reviews sometimes tend to be limited to answering questions such as, 'Why do you like this book?' This activity is designed to encourage them to think more closely about their reading. Rather than answering questions about the books they have read, the children are asked to prepare questions themselves.

Preparation

Look at the book which you are currently reading to the children and make up some questions about the text. These might be a mixture of factual questions and questions asking for people's opinions or predictions. Some questions might ask who did what when, while others may ask why something happened or what ought to happen to certain characters.

Resources needed

The class book that is being used as a current story for the children, the children's own reading books, writing materials.

What to do

Talk with the children about the book which you are currently reading to them and discuss the questions which you have posed about the class book. Explain that they are going to attempt the same thing with the books which they are currently reading themselves. Encourage them to produce a mixture of questions requiring factual answers, and questions which demand that the person answering the questions forms opinions. An example of the former might be 'What was the name of the policeman in *Danny, the Champion of the World?*' (Puffin, 1994) while the latter might include, 'Do you think that it was right that Danny and his father should poach Mr Hazell's pheasants? Explain your answer.'

Time which is set aside for quiet reading might be used for this activity, with children producing questions whenever they finish a book. The questions could be tucked inside the book for future readers to answer, either orally or in writing.

Suggestion(s) for extension

A book quiz could be organised, perhaps along *Mastermind* lines with children answering questions set by fellow pupils on their specialised subject – a book they have read recently or the books of a particular author.

Suggestion(s) for support

Children who find the activity difficult might be helped to formulate questions when they read to you or to an adult helper.

Assessment opportunities

Note children's abilities to write in an appropriate style for asking written questions, and look for evidence that they are able to use question marks correctly.

Opportunities for IT

The children could use a word processor to edit, organise and present a set of questions for the book they are reading. This could be done either as an ongoing activity, with children adding questions to a personal file as they think of new ones, or by children typing all of the questions they have noted down when they finish the book. The final list needs to be formatted so that it will fit into the back of the book.

Display ideas

A class book quiz display could be available for children to use when they complete work early.

Other aspects of the English PoS covered

Reading – 2b.

 # QUESTIONNAIRES

To use the features of layout and presentation of a questionnaire.

†† *Whole class or group, working individually.*

🕑 *One hour initially, but the activity may continue over a number of days as data is collected.*

Key background information

This activity is intended to develop children's abilities to make judgements about style and vocabulary in order to formulate questions which are unambiguous. It should also develop their abilities to analyse data and report, in writing, upon their findings.

Previous skills/knowledge needed

Children will need to understand terms such as 'surname', 'forename', 'address' and 'date of birth' which are included in questionnaires.

Preparation

Collect sample questionnaires. An example is the type found accompanying many brands of electrical goods, the questionnaires being used by manufacturers for market

research. Make copies of photocopiable pages 127 and 128 so that you have one questionnaire for each child. Cut out tables, charts and articles from newspapers so that the children can see how the results of questionnaires may be presented. Write the first part of a questionnaire on the board to use to introduce the 'development' section of the activity.

Resources needed

Sample questionnaires, tables, charts, articles (see above), photocopiable pages 127 and 128, chalkboard, black pens.

What to do

Introduction

Discuss with the children the purpose of a questionnaire. Show them the examples you have collected. Talk to the children about forms and ask them to find out from their parents about the sorts of forms adults have to complete. Talk about the instructions which are provided, such as those which ask for block capital letters, black ink, or ticking or circling of appropriate answers. Explain that forms are issued because different organisations need to gather information.

Development

Having introduced the idea of questionnaires and forms, show the children how you would complete a questionnaire, a part of which you have produced on the board. Discuss the need for brief but detailed answers to questions, and tell the children that they will usually need to use block capital letters when they fill in forms. Provide the children with the questionnaire on photocopiable pages 127 and 128 to complete.

Conclusion

Talk about the ways in which the results of questionnaires can be used. Show the children examples from newspapers and so on.

Suggestion(s) for extension

When the questionnaires have been completed appoint a small group to collate and present the results. Another group could analyse the results and write a commentary or a report for a class newspaper.

Suggestion(s) for support

It may be necessary to devise separate questionnaires for children who experience reading problems. Alternatively, children who find the exercise difficult might work with the assistance of a partner.

Assessment opportunities

Note the children's abilities to make suitable vocabulary choices and to write in an appropriate style for their audience.

Opportunities for IT

The children could create a computer database from their questionnaires, using the fieldnames from the questionnaire

WRITING

itself. Children can work in pairs or threes to enter the data, with one child checking the typing of the other child (or children) for accuracy and spellings.

It is important that children have sufficient time to use the completed database to answer questions that you or the children have prepared in advance. These could include sorts, which put the data into alphabetical or numerical order, simple searches on a single field and more complex ones using 'and' to narrow, or 'or' to widen the search. The questions should be framed to help children move from straightforward questions such as 'Which sport is played most often?' to more complex ones such as 'Do boys spend more time watching TV than girls?' or 'Is there any connection between reading and watching the TV?'

The children could be shown how to present their results using tables and a range of different graphs. They should also be asked to interpret their findings, explaining what the graphs show and what they have discovered.

Display ideas
The results of the questionnaires could be displayed with commentaries alongside them. A class newspaper could feature articles on the results.

Other aspects of the English PoS covered
Speaking and listening – 1a.
Reading – 1b.

Reference to photocopiable sheets
Photocopiable pages 127 and 128 provide a sample questionnaire for the children to complete.

Questionnaire (1)

Name _____ Date _____

▲ This questionnaire is intended to find information about children's leisure interests. All replies will be treated as confidential. Names and addresses are required for administrative purposes.

Please answer the following questions in black ink in block capital letters.

Full name _____

Gender (male/female) _____

Address _____

Street _____

Town _____ Postcode _____

Please answer the following questions by ticking the most suitable answers.
1 Which of these sports do you play in most weeks? (Please tick those which apply.)

☐ Athletics ☐ Hockey ☐ Tennis
☐ Cricket ☐ Judo ☐ Other (please state)
☐ Football ☐ Netball _____
☐ Golf ☐ Rounders _____
☐ Gymnastics ☐ Rugby ☐ None

2 How many hours do you spend watching television on an average school day? (Please tick one.)

☐ Less than 1 hour ☐ Between 3 and 4 hours
☐ Between 1 and 2 hours ☐ More than 4 hours
☐ Between 2 and 3 hours

Thank you for taking the time and trouble to answer the questions.

PLAYGROUND GAMES

To produce accurate non-fiction writing in an appropriate style.

†† *Whole class or group, working individually.*

🕐 *At least one hour.*

Key background information
In this activity children write descriptions of the games which they play in the playground, including rules and interesting features. The writing is therefore descriptive and explanatory as well as instructional.

Preparation
Tell the children in advance that they will be doing some work about playground games and encourage them to ask other children about the games they play.

Resources needed
Writing materials.

What to do
Talk with the children about the games they play in the playground and ask them to describe how the games are played and to mention any rules. There may well be disputes over rules, with different children playing different versions of the same game. (Use this as a reason for asking them to write instructions for their version.) If you played the games in a different way as a child, tell them about your own versions. Explain that the children are going to write a description of the games and then instructions for how to play. Encourage them to draft their work and to revise and proofread it.

Suggestion(s) for extension
Children could be encouraged to talk to parents, grandparents and other adults about the games which they played as children. Descriptions of these games could be written by the children and a class display or book could be produced.

Suggestion(s) for support
Children who need help with spellings and so on should be assisted, but notes should be made about the extent to which children were able to work independently.

Assessment opportunities
Look for evidence that children are able to adopt appropriate styles for descriptive writing and for writing instructions, and that they are able to draft and revise their work to improve accuracy.

Other aspects of the English PoS covered
Speaking and listening – 1a; 2b.

WRITING

Language study

In this chapter children are provided with activities which focus on the development of their understanding of the English language. There are opportunities to extend their knowledge of the metalanguage which can be so useful in discussing their work. Some activities, for example, involve the use of terms such as adverb, simile, pronoun and conjunction. In the past some educators fought shy of introducing such terminology, but, while knowledge of terminology does not of itself improve children's writing, it does enable them to gain an insight into the devices which they might use in order to develop and improve it.

Some of the activities take the form of exercises designed to reinforce learning, but most require an element of creativity. There is an emphasis on the development of accurate punctuation and on ways in which punctuation may be used to improve the structure of writing. Some of the activities are intended to foster an interest in vocabulary and to broaden children's knowledge of the wealth of possibilities which exist when making word choices. There are also activities which focus on different ways of using language, and on the differences between written and spoken English.

Ultimately, the purpose of writing is to offer a means of clear communication. An understanding of the structures of the English language and experience of their use should help to develop this in young writers.

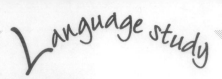

SENTENCES AND FULL STOPS

To use full stops accurately.

†† *Whole class, working individually, then in pairs.*

🕐 *At least one hour.*

Previous skills/knowledge needed

The children should have some awareness of the fact that written and spoken English conform to different rules. They should be able to communicate meaning through simple words and phrases in their own writing. They should understand the functions of capital letters.

Key background information

In this activity the children will learn that a sentence can be described as a set of words making a single complete statement and that it begins with a capital letter and ends with a full stop.

Preparation

Prepare a short and simple passage of unpunctuated writing. This could either be something composed by you or another piece of writing adapted for the purpose – a set of instructions or directions would make particularly good exemplar material. It is essential that the chosen piece of writing should be capable of division into short, unambiguous sentences. There should be a copy of the piece for each child. Arrange to have a room with enough uncluttered space for the children to walk around safely! The school hall or gym would be the most suitable space. For those children requiring support work, prepare a display version of your chosen passage, correctly punctuated, on a large sheet of A3 paper. Write each sentence in a different coloured ink. For the extension activity prepare copies of a poem with several verses.

Resources needed

A passage of unpunctuated writing, a large room (see above). For the extension activity – copies of a poem with several verses. For the support activity – a sheet of A3 paper and felt-tipped pens to make an enlarged correctly punctuated version of the passage of writing you are using.

What to do

Explain to the children that readers do not have the verbal and aural clues which listeners rely on in order to make sense of what someone is saying. Readers do not have any visual clues either. Sentences are one of the means by which writers can make sure their meaning is understood.

Give the children their copy of the unpunctuated writing. Line them up against a wall. On the command 'Go!' they are to start walking towards the opposite wall, reading the passage as they go. They must neither pause for breath nor stop walking till they finish the passage (hence the need to keep the piece of writing brief!). Bring the class together and draw on their comments about the exercise to emphasise the fact that punctuation brings sense and order to writing.

Ask the children to repeat the walking/reading exercise. This time, however, they must try to work out where the missing full stops are (it helps if you tell them how many they have to find). Every time they locate a full stop, they are to stop walking and pause for breath. When they start a new sentence, they start walking again in a new direction.

Move the pupils into pairs. Give each pair five minutes to compare their findings and prepare a joint reading of the passage and an explanation of what it is about. Encourage them to justify their choice of full-stop pauses to each other and to compare the number of full stops they found. If they disagree, so much the better; but they must eventually come to a consensus. Bring the children together again to discuss the issues arising as a whole group.

Suggestion(s) for extension

Once the children have grasped the idea, you can try the exercises again, this time using more adventurous material such as a verse of a poem. Alternatively, different groups could work on different verses of the same poem so that the whole class could eventually produce a choral presentation of the piece for assembly. Variations on the 'walking/reading' idea could include saying each sentence in a different tone of voice or with a different action.

Suggestion(s) for support

Show the children the enlarged version of the short piece of writing which you have punctuated correctly. Explain to the children exactly why you placed the full stops where you did. Put the sheet on the wall for future reference. This explanation might be followed by the children being given a brief passage to punctuate in order to reinforce learning.

Assessment opportunities

Use the walking/reading exercises and the presentations to assess how well the children have grasped the concept of the use of sentences in writing.

Display ideas

Ask the children to design a poster which will remind children at the school (older as well as younger) of the purpose of sentences and full stops. Can they think of a memorable sentence, picture and caption which will help the information 'stick'? Display the posters around the school.

Other aspects of the English PoS covered

Speaking and listening – 2a; 3a.
Reading – 3.

FOUR-LETTER WORDS

To produce a bank of four-letter words which are spelled correctly.
†† *Individuals or pairs.*
🕐 *One hour.*

Key background information

This activity is intended to encourage familiarity with common four-letter words (of the non-expletive sort!) and to encourage children to make use of dictionaries.

Preparation

Make a collection of words with four letters which might be introduced if the children need an additional vocabulary source. You can use photocopiable page 129 which provides a useful source. The children will need one copy each or one per pair.

Resources needed

Dictionaries, photocopiable page 129, writing materials. A short list of four-letter words for support activity.

What to do

Ask the children to list as many words with four letters as they can. This could be an activity to be done immediately after a break to settle the children down quickly. After a short time ask them to exchange lists and use dictionaries to check spellings. Give out copies of photocopiable page 129 on which they can add four-letter words which are not already listed.

Talk to the children about the difference between common and proper nouns and ask them to look for examples of each in their lists.

Encourage the children to use dictionaries to find more four-letter words. Tell them that they will need to be able to use the words in sentences eventually so it is important that they know what the words mean.

Ask the children to use the four-letter words they have found in a piece of writing. They might be asked to write a 100-word story with as many as possible of the words having four letters. They could compare the percentage of four-letter words in their work with the percentage in samples of literature.

Suggestion(s) for extension

Similar activities could be undertaken with words of other lengths. Children could take collections of four-letter words and make alphabetical lists for display in the classroom.

Suggestion(s) for support

The children could be presented with a short list of four-letter words to help them to get started on the activity.

Assessment opportunities

Note the children's abilities to make use of dictionaries and to use vocabulary appropriately in their stories.

WRITING

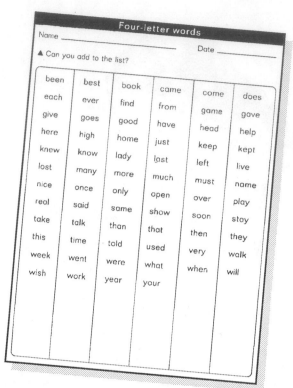

Four-letter words

Name _____ Date _____

▲ Can you add to the list?

been	best	book	came	come	does
each	ever	find	from	game	gave
give	goes	good	have	head	help
here	high	home	just	keep	kept
knew	know	lady	last	left	live
lost	many	more	much	must	name
nice	once	only	open	over	play
real	said	same	show	soon	stay
take	talk	than	that	then	they
this	time	told	used	very	walk
week	went	were	what	when	will
wish	work	year	your		

Opportunities for IT

Children could use the spelling dictionary or thesaurus connected to their word processor, or a hand-held spelling checker, to look for four-letter words.

Display ideas

Display lists of words of different lengths and encourage children to add to these. If the words are displayed on individual pieces of card, children can be asked to put them into alphabetical order and continue to do this as new words are added.

Other aspects of the English PoS covered

Reading – 2c.

Reference to photocopiable sheet

Photocopiable page 129 provides a list of four-letter words which the children can add their own words to.

COMBINING SENTENCES

To make use of conjunctions to link sentences.

†† *Individuals or pairs.*

⊕ *30–40 minutes.*

Key background information

In this activity the children are given a list of short sentences on a particular theme which they are asked to combine into fewer, but longer, sentences. Conjunctions such as 'and', 'but', 'so' and 'then' are sometimes overused in children's writing, but often writing includes a lot of short sentences, some of which might be combined by using conjunctions in order to make writing flow more easily. The activity focuses attention on conjunctions and their usage.

Preparation

Prepare on the board a list of short sentences which can be joined using conjunctions. Photocopy page 130, one copy for each child or pair. Prepare a list of longer sentences (which can be joined by conjunctions) for the extension activity.

Resources needed

A list of short sentences (see above), photocopiable page 130, writing materials, chalkboard. *Breakthrough to Literacy* materials (by David Mackay *et al.*, Longman) for the support activity. A list of longer sentences for the extension activity.

What to do

Show the children a list of short sentences and ask them to combine the sentences orally to reduce the number but increase the length of the sentences. After a few attempts write the children's suggestions on the board and discuss the ways in which they have achieved the aim. Talk about 'joining words' (conjunctions) and the role that they play.

Show the children the photocopiable sheet and explain that they are going to try to combine the sentences. Ask them if they can halve the number of sentences in each section without changing the meaning.

As the children work, discuss with them the different ways in which they have approached the task and emphasise that there is no one correct answer for each section.

It is important to reiterate the need for capital letters and full stops.

Suggestion(s) for extension

Provide longer lists of sentences and invite the children to make the writing more interesting and imaginative, possibly by adding adverbs and adjectives.

Suggestion(s) for support

Breakthrough to Literacy materials might be used to help children to manipulate the words physically before writing them down.

Assessment opportunities

Note the children's abilities to write coherent and correctly punctuated sentences.

Opportunities for IT

Prepare the passage in advance, using a word processor, so that the children can then use the editing features of the word processor to join sentences.

Combining sentences

Date _____

Name _____

▲ Can you join the sentences in each group so that there are fewer sentences? You may add words or take words away.

Group 1
Dominic has a bicycle.
Sophie has a bicycle.
Raj has a football.
Nicola has a tennis ball.

Group 2
The wind blew.
The rain fell heavily.
Asif was fast asleep.
Lee could not sleep.

Group 3
The dog awoke.
It scratched itself.
It shook itself.
The dog went to look for something to eat.
There was nothing in its bowl.
The dog began to bark.

Group 4
Harold and his men looked down on William's men from the top of the hill.
William had a cunning plan.
William's men fired arrows high into the air.
One of the arrows hit Harold.
Harold was killed.
William's army had won the battle.

Display ideas

Groups of short sentences could be displayed for children to use for further work in this area.

Other aspects of the English PoS covered

Speaking and listening – 3a.

Reference to photocopiable sheet

Photocopiable page 130 provides examples of short sentences which the children are asked to combine to make longer sentences.

UNFINISHED SENTENCES

To demonstrate an understanding of sentence structure.

†† *Whole class or group, working individually or in pairs.*

🕐 *30–40 minutes.*

Key background information

This activity is designed to heighten children's awareness of the concept of the sentence, while allowing them to write imaginatively.

Preparation

Write examples of incomplete sentences on the board. Make copies of photocopiable page 131, either one for each child or one per pair. On a sheet of A4 paper write a set of unfinished sentences using simpler vocabulary than those on photocopiable page 131 for children who need support work. Photocopy the A4 sheet, one copy for each child.

Resources needed

Photocopiable page 131, writing materials, chalkboard. A4 sheets of easy-to-read incomplete sentences for support activity.

What to do

Provide examples of incomplete sentences on the board and discuss with the children what will be needed to complete the sentences. Discuss with the children the importance of punctuating sentences correctly with capital letters and full stops. Provide some examples to show that failure to do so can lead to confusion. For example, the same words can convey different meanings if full stops and capital letters are placed differently:

> At Christmas Hayley was going to buy lots of things for herself. She was going to buy nothing for everyone else. It was going to be a wonderful time.
>
> At Christmas Hayley was going to buy lots of things. For herself, she was going to buy nothing. For everyone else it was going to be a wonderful time.

Talk with the children about what a sentence is. It should say something about a person or a thing. Talk about some of the incomplete sentences and ask what is missing.

Give out the photocopiable sheets and explain to the children that they will need to complete the sentences. Encourage them to be imaginative in their choice of endings, and stop them regularly as they work to read aloud examples of interesting sentences.

Suggestion(s) for extension

Children could work in pairs, writing incomplete sentences for each other to complete. They might move on to providing the endings of sentences for partners to write beginnings.

WRITING

Unfinished sentences

Name _____ Date _____

▲ Can you complete the sentences? Try to make the sentences as interesting as possible.

1 The car's tyres screeched as _____

2 A gust of wind picked up the baseball cap and _____

3 I don't care if I never _____

4 Ben felt himself falling as he _____

5 Holly opened the sack and pulled out a _____

6 Every eye in the room looked at him as he _____

7 My favourite game is_____

8 The noise was deafening, but Rebecca knew she had to _____

9 Although he was often silly, Nicholas was _____

10 I made sure no one was looking and then I _____

Opportunities for IT
You could produce a set of unfinished sentences in advance, so that the children can write their own endings using the word processor.

Display ideas
Display incomplete sentences from books and invite the children to complete them before comparing them with what the authors wrote.

Other aspects of the English PoS covered
Reading – 3.

Reference to photocopiable sheet
Photocopiable page 131 is comprised of sentences which are unfinished and which the children can complete.

QUESTION MARKS

To use question marks accurately.
♥♥ *Whole class, individuals/pairs and small group work.*
🕐 *At least one hour.*

Suggestion(s) for support
A set of incomplete sentences with simpler vocabulary could be provided for children who encounter difficulty in reading those on photocopiable page 131.

Assessment opportunities
Look for correct punctuation, interesting choices of vocabulary, and an understanding of the concept of the sentence.

Previous skills/knowledge needed
Children should understand that writing can be organised into sentences and that sentences begin with a capital letter and usually end with a full stop.

Key background information
Direct questions are sentences or phrases which require an answer. They often begin with the words 'Why', 'What', 'Where', 'When' and 'How'. *Indirect questions* are reported

questions which do not require a direct answer. For example: 'She asked me what the time was.' 'Question marks' is comprised of three activities which focus on direct and indirect questions. The activities should be attempted consecutively.

Preparation
Make copies of photocopiable page 132, one copy for each child.

Resources needed
Meet My Folks! by Ted Hughes (Faber & Faber, 1987), photocopiable page 132, writing materials. For support activity – an A4 sheet containing direct and indirect questions (see 'Suggestion(s) for support'), word processor/cassette player and blank cassettes.

What to do
These are three activities which should be attempted consecutively.

The Question Game
Ask the children some questions, for example: 'How are you? What time is it? How old are you?' Use their responses to make the point that we recognise questions by the fact that they demand an answer. Repeat the exercise, this time asking only indirect questions. Draw on the fact that the children do not answer you this time to point out the rule about indirect questions.

Now ask the children to stand in a circle. Explain the rules of 'The Question Game'. Two people face each other in the middle of the circle. They are allowed to ask each other only direct questions. For example, if the first person says, 'What time is it?' the second person might reply, 'Who wants to know?' The dialogue continues until one person fails to respond with a question. This person drops out of the circle and is replaced by another challenger. The person left standing in the middle of the circle at the end is the winner. As the children become more confident with the game, try to speed up the questions so that they have to listen very carefully to each other if they want to stay 'in'.

Twenty Questions
Divide the children into teams of three or four. Give each team a 'crazy occupation' – the more imaginative, the better! Ted Hughes's poetry collection *Meet My Folks!* is a good source of inspiration. Keeping their occupation secret from the others, each team prepares a brief mime (no more than 60 seconds) to illustrate their occupation. The mime should be as literal and as detailed as possible. After each performance, each watching team is allowed to put five questions to the members of the performing team. The questions must be direct questions requiring only 'yes' or 'no' answers. Make sure that each team is allowed to go

first at least once. The team which guesses the most occupations correctly is the winner. Points are deducted for incorrect questions.

What was the Question?
Give each child a copy of photocopiable page 132. Ask the children to write out questions which they imagine best suit each of the answers. Invite the children to read out their favourites and ask the class to choose the one which they think is the most imaginative and/or exciting.

Suggestion(s) for extension
Ask the children to swap their own favourite question from the 'What was the Question?' activity with that of a partner. They can then write a short story which begins with and is based upon the question their partner has given them. The question should provide the title of the story.

Suggestion(s) for support
Children who lack confidence to play the 'The Question Game' as individuals could challenge in pairs or trios and be given time to prepare a list of possible questions. All children could be given an aide-mémoire sheet containing the points described in 'Key background information' and supported by clear examples such as 'How did you spend your pocket

money?' 'Why have you come to school early today?' (direct) and 'He asked her how she spent her pocket money', 'She asked him why he had come to school early' (indirect). Less able writers might compose a joint story for 'What was the Question?', using a word processor or a cassette player. Alternatively, you or a classroom helper could act as scribe for the children.

Assessment opportunities
The games 'The Question Game' and 'Twenty Questions' provide opportunities for oral assessment. The children's grasp of the concepts can be assessed through their written response to the activity 'What was the Question?' The questions which they write in response to the 'answers' given in 'What was the Question?' will also provide an opportunity to assess their ability to 'read between the lines'.

Display ideas
Newspapers, magazines and advertisements make particular and lively use of questions in their attempts to engage the reader. Assemble an eye-catching collage of your favourites and display these on the classroom wall. Label one or two with your own comments, explaining how you feel they are used by the writers to arouse the curiosity of the reader.

Other aspects of the English PoS covered
Speaking and listening – 1a, c; 2b; 3a, b.
Writing – 1c; 2a, c.

Reference to photocopiable sheet
Photocopiable page 132 provides a list of answers for which the children write appropriate questions.

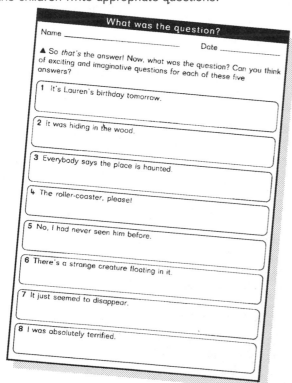

What was the question?

Name _____
Date _____

▲ So *that's* the answer! Now, what was the question? Can you think of exciting and imaginative questions for each of these five answers?

1 It's Lauren's birthday tomorrow.

2 It was hiding in the wood.

3 Everybody says the place is haunted.

4 The roller-coaster, please!

5 No, I had never seen him before.

6 There's a strange creature floating in it.

7 It just seemed to disappear.

8 I was absolutely terrified.

COMMAS

To use commas correctly in sentences.
†† *Whole class, working in small groups.*
🕐 *At least one hour.*

Previous skills/knowledge needed
Children need to be aware of basic sentence structure. They should know how to use the punctuation marks which separate sentences from each other: full stops, exclamation marks, question marks. It would also help if they were familiar with the following parts of speech: noun, verb, adjective, adverb, preposition, conjunction.

Key background information
In this activity the children will learn that the comma is used in sentences to separate words, phrases and some clauses. The comma separates:
▲ words in a list
(It was a dark, stormy, frightening night.)
▲ (in direct speech) the name of the person being addressed from the rest of the sentence
('Jane, I'd like a word with you.')
▲ an adverbial from the rest of the sentence
('Sadly, we shall not see him till Tuesday.')

Preparation
Look through newspapers, magazines and comics for interesting examples of commas in use. The best ones are those where the inclusion or removal of the comma would change the meaning of the sentence. Advertisements and

newspaper headlines are a particularly useful source of information because of their reliance on wordplay.

Familiarise yourself with the story 'The comma that saved a human life' on photocopiable page 133 and photocopy this sheet for every child in the class. Make copies of photocopiable page 134, one for each group.

Resources needed

A personal collection of printed material illustrating the various uses of the comma (see 'Preparation'), photocopiable pages 133 and 134, chalkboard, writing materials. Labels and highlighter/marker pens for the support activity.

What to do

Explain to the children that commas separate units of sense *within* rather than *between* sentences. Like full stops, commas allow the reader to 'take a breather', though one which is shorter.

Gather the children around you and tell them the story of 'The comma that saved a human life' on photocopiable page 133. Use the story to impress upon the children the importance of accurate punctuation in writing. Once you have told the children the story, give out the copies of photocopiable page 133. Write the climactic lines of the story, containing the two key sentences, on the board, so that all the children can appreciate the way the comma alters the meaning and see how important the placing of the comma is.

Using the exemplar material you collected before the lesson, explain to the children the rules about the use of the comma outlined in 'Key background information'.

Organise the class into groups of three. Give each group photocopiable page 134 which provides a selection of sentences which need punctuating with commas. The children have to supply the missing commas.

Suggestion(s) for extension

Help the children to analyse and question each other's exemplar material from the point of view of a person who speaks English as a second language.

Suggestion(s) for support

Make an eye-catching collage of the newsprint material you collected earlier (see 'Preparation'). Use labels, arrows, a marker pen and so on to highlight and explain instances of the comma in use. Explain to the children how the collage works, display it in the classroom and encourage them to consult it for help when in difficulties.

Assessment opportunities

Examine the work the children produce and look particularly at the quality of their explanations of the comma rules they are trying to describe. Listen carefully, too, to the questions they ask about each other's exemplar material.

Opportunities for IT

The children could use a word processor or drawing package to design a poster, giving examples and explanations of the different uses of commas.

Other aspects of the English PoS covered

Speaking and listening – 2b.
Reading – 2c.

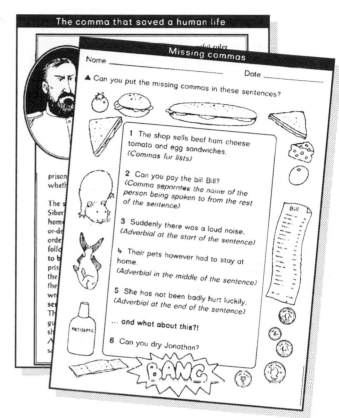

Reference to photocopiable sheets

The story on photocopiable page 133 shows children the importance of where commas are placed. On photocopiable page 134 the children punctuate the sentences, all of which require commas.

EXCLAMATION MARKS

To use exclamation marks appropriately.

Whole class, then groups of four children.

At least one hour.

Previous skills/knowledge needed

Children need to have some awareness of the relationship between punctuation and meaning in written language. They should at least be familiar with the use of capital letters and full stops in sentences.

Key background information

In this activity children will learn that exclamation marks are used to indicate statements which express excitement or arousal of some kind, for example fear, surprise, joy, anger and urgency. Exclamatory statements often begin with 'What' or 'How'. For example: 'What a load of rubbish!', 'How dare you!'

Resources needed

Writing and drawing materials, cassette player and blank cassettes (optional).

What to do

Focus the children on the activity by helping them to think about the ways in which intonation can alter the meaning of speech. A good way to do this is to ask the children to sit in a circle and then 'pass' a word round the group. Each person has to try to say the word in a totally different tone of voice – loudly, angrily, softly, timidly, humorously, craftily and so on. The rule is that each version must be an exclamation of some kind.

Divide the children into groups of four and give each group a sheet of A4 paper. Tell them that you want each group to script a radio play. The play must be no more than 60 seconds long (be strict about this!). The children are only allowed to use sound effects and exclamatory statements (one per child). The theme of the play can be funny or exciting or mysterious.

Example of a possible script extract:

SEAN	What on earth!
(sound of door creaking)	
LUCY	Don't panic, Sean!
SEAN	Help! There's something out there!
LUCY	Stop being silly! You're frightening me!
SEAN	I can't help it! Listen!
(The children are silent for a few seconds. The door creaks again.)	
SEAN	You must believe me!
LUCY	Yes I do! Quick, telephone the police!
SEAN	There's no time! Let's get out of here while we can!

Once the children have written out their script and had it checked by you, give each group a cassette player and cassette. The children can then record the play 'live' in one 'take'. Alternatively, they can rehearse their script for subsequent performance in front of the class.

Once all the plays have been recorded or rehearsed together, gather the whole class to listen to the recordings (or to watch the plays) and discuss how well the exclamatory statements succeeded in creating a sense of atmosphere, engaging the audience and conveying the play's theme.

Finally, after the plays have been performed, ask each child to choose one exclamatory statement from his or her favourite play, write it out in large letters on a sheet of A4 (plus exclamation mark!) and draw a picture to illustrate the scene. Encourage each child to add a sentence at the bottom of the sheet explaining why that particular statement required an exclamation mark.

Suggestion(s) for extension

Some children may enjoy designing an advertising poster for a product of their choice. However, give them the rule that they must use a total of five exclamation marks, with each exclamation mark representing a different tone of voice.

Suggestion(s) for support

Less confident children should be given a clear, dramatic story-line to work on for their plays. Some children may wish to design a poster in pairs or trios.

Assessment opportunities

Note the children's abilities to use exclamation marks appropriately. Note, too, their success in adopting an appropriate format for script writing.

Opportunities for IT

The children could use a drawing or art package to make a poster about their statements which contain exclamation marks. They could also experiment with different fonts, colours and letter sizes to create a visual display of a particular word or phrase which has an exclamation mark, perhaps using a drawing package to bend and shape the letters into different forms. The word 'halt!', for example, could have the four letters of the word overlapping each other.

74

Display ideas

Put up a display of words, phrases and clauses, each with an exclamation mark. These should be written on individual pieces of card. Provide blank pieces of card and thick felt-tipped pens so that children can add to the display as they find examples of exclamation marks in their reading.

Other aspects of the English PoS covered

Speaking and listening – 1a; 2b; 3b.

SPEECH BUBBLES

To use speech marks accurately.

†† *Individuals.*

🕐 *One hour.*

Key background information

This activity is designed to develop children's abilities to use speech marks.

Preparation

Look at examples of comics and comic-strip stories with the children. Photocopy some comic strips and blank out the words in the speech bubbles. This can be done with sticky labels.

Resources needed

Comic strips without speech (see above), writing materials. Comics for the extension activity.

What to do

Show the children one of the blank comic strips and discuss what the characters might be saying. Write in some of their suggestions and show them how these can be written in reported speech. Ask them to look at their reading books and see how speech is reported. They may find some examples of single inverted commas and some of double inverted commas depending upon the style of the print. It is important that they know that either is acceptable.

Show the children how the speech in the bubbles can be written and encourage them to try for themselves. When you feel that they are sufficiently confident, ask them to fill in the speech bubbles on another cartoon strip and then transcribe them into reported speech. Emphasise the importance of reporting who says what, and discuss alternatives to 'he said' and 'she said'.

As the children work, it may become apparent that they are unsure of where to place punctuation marks and when to use capital letters. Encourage them to look at published texts so that they can see how the authors have punctuated speech. You could use short mnemonics to help the children remember how to punctuate direct speech. For example, '66, capital, 1 of 4, 99' reminds us that the initial inverted commas resemble the number 66 and that these are followed by a capital letter, then one of the four punctuation marks ? ! , . and then the final inverted commas which resemble the number 99.

Suggestion(s) for extension

Provide comics for the children to transcribe the speech in the bubbles into reported speech.

Suggestion(s) for support

Children who struggle with the activity could take a piece of unpunctuated writing and underline or circle the speech as an introduction to using inverted commas.

Assessment opportunities

Note the children's abilities to punctuate speech accurately.

Display ideas

Display comic strips and invite children to transcribe these when they have time to spare or when they have completed other activities.

Other aspects of the English PoS covered

Reading – 3.

WRITING

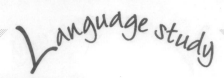

PARAGRAPHS

To use paragraphs accurately.

Whole class, working in small groups.

At least one hour.

Previous skills/knowledge needed

The children should understand how writing is organised into sentences and should be familiar with the layout of text on a page. They should also have some grasp of the concept that narratives have a 'beginning', a 'middle' and an 'ending'.

Key background information

In this activity the children study the function of paragraphs in writing. They will learn that new paragraphs should be started for changes in time, place, subject and speaker.

Preparation

Cut copies of photocopiable page 135 into three sections (one per paragraph) to give one section to each member of your three groups (see 'What to do').

Resources needed

Photocopiable page 135, writing and drawing materials, chalkboard, scrap paper, scissors. For support activity – cassette player and blank cassettes (optional). For extension activity – reading material to show use of paragraphs.

What to do

Explain to the children how and why writers organise their work into paragraphs. Tell them that organising writing into paragraphs makes it easier to read and better presented.

Divide the class into groups of three and give each member of the group one of the three paragraphs comprising the 'Stepping-stones story' on photocopiable page 135. Tell each member of the group to read his or her paragraph to the other two children. The listeners then make notes on what the reader says and draw a simple picture for each paragraph which includes as much of the information they have heard as possible. Placing the pictures beside their corresponding paragraphs, the children try to decide among themselves why the author of the passage chose to divide the text in this way. Invite the various groups to share their ideas through whole class discussion. Record the main points on the board.

Working in trios again, invite the children to rearrange the paragraphs in the following sequences: 1, 2, 3; 3, 2,1; 2, 3, 1. Ask them to consider the following questions:

▲ How does the meaning of the text alter each time?

▲ Are there certain words or phrases which only seem right when placed at the start or at the end of the sequence? Why is this?

Allow the children to discuss these points in their trios initially, and then draw the main ideas together through a teacher-led whole class discussion. When the story is assembled with the paragraphs in the correct order the following questions can be considered when summing up:

▲ Why do the paragraph breaks come where they do?

▲ How was the impact of the story changed when the paragraphs were assembled in a different order?

▲ Do specific words and phrases play a particularly important part in deciding the sequence?

Stepping-stones Game

Introduce the activity to the children like this:

'We are going to continue our work on paragraphs by playing the 'Stepping-stones Game'. I want you to imagine that a story is like stepping-stones across a river. The beginning of the story is one bank of the river. The ending of the story is on the opposite bank. To get from one bank to the other, we have to put three stepping-stones across the river. Each of these stepping-stones is a paragraph of our story.'

Divide the children into teams of four composed of two groups of two. Group 1 of each team takes the opening paragraph of the 'Stepping-stones story' and develops a *new* story from this starting point by adding two *original* paragraphs (three 'stepping-stones' in all). Group 2 of each team takes the final paragraph of the story and composes two *original* paragraphs to make an interesting 'lead-in' to the ending (three 'stepping-stones' in all). The rule is that, although the beginnings and endings of the story are the same, the other paragraphs must be different from those in the original extract. The two groups will work independently of each other at this stage. It might be helpful to remind the

WRITING

children that the story on photocopiable page 135 begins like a horror story and has a humorous 'twist in the tale' at the end. Are they going to try to imitate this style, choose 'straight' horror or comedy, or go for something different altogether?

Tell group 1 and group 2 to sketch out the development of their three paragraphs on scrap paper. Then ask them to write out their paragraphs of the story (still in rough). After consulting their partners and agreeing that the three paragraphs run smoothly together, the 'beginning' and 'ending' pairs read each other's work. Do the 'stepping-stones' meet in the middle of the 'river'?

Open up the activity to whole class discussion. Invite various teams to read out their stories and to comment on whether they match or not. Use this part of the lesson as an opportunity to reinforce the uses of paragraphing and to consider whether the children matched the style of the original story or changed it.

Invite each group of four to rework their stories so that the openings and endings do 'meet in the middle'. Do they need to revise the whole story, or will the reworking of one paragraph be enough to make a match? When the children feel that their writing has been sufficiently revised, they can write out the final version of their stories.

Suggestion(s) for extension

Children can be encouraged to look at chapters in books and identify the paragraph changes. They can then go on to note the reasons for each change, for example: time, place, subject or speaker.

Suggestion(s) for support

The children could make a tape of their 'Stepping-stones story' or represent it in a series of pictures. Their comments on the drafting process could also be recorded on tape.

Assessment opportunities

The children's grasp of the concept of paragraphing can be assessed through their written contributions to the 'Stepping-stones story' and through their oral contributions to the small group and whole class discussion sessions. Children could also be asked to provide a written or taped commentary on their reasons for structuring their paragraphs as they did (see 'Suggestion(s) for support').

Opportunities for IT

If the opening or closing paragraphs are available as word-processed files, these can be selected by the children and inserted into their own work to save having to retype them. Alternatively, the children could begin with a file containing all of the paragraphs (numbered to aid recognition) and then use the editing features to remove paragraphs they do not want, or to help them reorder them as appropriate for their activity.

Display ideas

The rough notes and the finished 'Stepping-stones story' sheets could make an effective visual display designed to remind children about the drafting process and about narrative structure.

Other aspects of the English PoS covered

Speaking and listening – 1a, c; 2a, b; 3b.
Reading – 1a, c; 2b, c; 3.

Reference to photocopiable sheet

Photocopiable page 135 may be copied and cut into three paragraphs for use in the main activity.

PRONOUNS

To use pronouns appropriately to enhance writing.

†† *Small groups/pairs or individuals.*

🕐 *One hour.*

Key background information

Children often repeat names of characters in their writing, when pronouns would make their writing more interesting and less repetitive. This activity is designed to encourage them to consider alternatives to the repetition of names and the use of common pronouns such as 'he', 'she' and 'it'.

Preparation

Make copies of photocopiable page 136, enough for one for each child or pair.

WRITING

Pronouns

▲ Read the passage below. How could it be improved? Write your new version on a separate sheet of paper.

Jenny was always smiling. Jenny was a very happy little girl and Jenny was never sad. Jenny had a brother called Daniel. Daniel was younger than Jenny. Daniel smiled a lot, but sometimes Daniel cried when he wanted some milk or when his nappy needed to be changed.

Jenny's mummy and daddy were very happy too. Her mummy was a bus driver. Jenny's mummy drove big double-decker buses. Jenny's daddy worked in a factory. Jenny's daddy helped to make cars. Jenny wanted to make buses when she grew up.

▲ Can you use pronouns to improve this piece of writing about Robert and Rover? Use a separate sheet of paper.

Robert's dog was called Rover. Robert really liked Rover. Robert used to take Rover into the park and throw sticks for him. Rover refused to fetch the sticks back to Robert so Robert tried throwing balls instead. Rover would not fetch balls either and Robert lost a lot of balls playing with Rover.

Robert tried to teach Rover other tricks. Robert tried to teach Rover to sit up and beg. Rover would not sit up and beg. Robert tried to teach Rover to fetch the newspaper from the shop, but Rover just lay in front of the fire.

Some people said that Rover was not a very clever dog because he would not run around fetching things and because he would not sit up and beg. Robert thought that Rover was very clever because he would not run around fetching things and because he would not sit up and beg.

Resources needed
Photocopiable page 136, writing materials. Children's reading books for extension activity.

What to do
Read the first example from the photocopiable sheet and ask the children what they think could be done to improve it. This section might be attempted orally by the whole group, or it could be done by the children writing in pairs or as individuals after it has been introduced and some of the work has been done collectively.

Ask the children to make use of pronouns in their writing to improve the second piece (either in pairs or individually). Let them share their ideas with the rest of the group.

Now ask the children to write about a friend or a relative. Give them clear ideas about what they should include in their writing. These might include:
▲ appearance;
▲ hobbies;
▲ personality;
▲ friends;
▲ likes and dislikes.
Tell the children that they must mention the person's name as little as possible in their writing and that they should use pronouns to replace the name wherever possible, providing the passage still makes sense. Encourage them to draft and edit their work.

Suggestion(s) for extension
Ask the children to look in their reading books for pronouns. Ask them to note, in particular, examples of phrases being used to replace a name: for example, the use of 'the little girl' or 'the frightened man' instead of a name.

Suggestion(s) for support
Children might work in pairs for mutual support. In order to reinforce the idea of pronouns it may be worth listening to children reading, and asking them to spot pronouns in the text.

Assessment opportunities
Note evidence that children understand the function of pronouns and are able to use them to make their writing more interesting.

Display ideas
Make a display of the children's writing and let them use highlighter pens to mark the pronouns. Display a collection of pronouns alongside the work.

Other aspects of the English PoS covered
Reading – 3.

Reference to photocopiable sheet
Photocopiable page 136 provides two pieces of writing which the children can improve through the use of pronouns.

▣ TRUE OR FALSE?

To write clear definitions of words.
†† *Group of children, working co-operatively in small groups.*
🕐 *Up to one hour.*

Previous skills/knowledge needed
Children will need to have some familiarity with the structure of dictionaries and the ways in which definitions are presented.

Key background information
In this activity the children play a game in which they offer definitions of an unfamiliar word, only one of which is a true definition. The children can work in groups of three or four, using dictionaries to find unusual words. After choosing these words, the children prepare some true and false definitions to challenge their classmates.

Preparation
Show the children how the game is played by preparing your own definitions and asking the children to decide which ones they think are true and why.

Resources needed
Dictionaries, writing materials. (The dictionaries should be accessible to the children, but should be more comprehensive than many of the simplified versions which are designed for primary-aged pupils.)

What to do

Having explained the game to the children, look with them at the dictionaries and find an unfamiliar word. Ask them to think of false definitions for it and let them try these out on other children in the class.

When you feel that the children are capable of working independently, and when they have understood the abbreviations and structure in the dictionary definitions, ask them to work in their groups to produce definitions for a series of words.

When they have prepared their definitions, let them try them out on the rest of the class. Explain that the other children must say why they believe the definitions are true or false.

Suggestion(s) for extension

Children could produce dictionaries of unusual words with definitions, as well as dictionaries of false definitions. A class dictionary could be produced.

Suggestion(s) for support

Some children may need to work closely with members of their group to produce definitions, but the activity is intended to be done co-operatively.

Assessment opportunities

Note the children's abilities to explain the meanings of words.

Opportunities for IT

The children could use a word processor to draft out their dictionary definitions. They could use different fonts and

styles to help them present their work in a dictionary format. The individual definitions could be printed out for display or used (as in the 'Suggestions for extension') to make a class dictionary, with the addition of features such as headwords.

Display ideas

Definitions could be displayed for other classes to look at and determine by reading them which ones they think are true and which false.

Other aspects of the English PoS covered

Reading – 2c.
Speaking and listening – 1a, b, c; 2a, b.

💻 DIALECT AND STANDARD ENGLISH: 1

To understand how written standard English often differs from spoken dialect.
👥 *Whole class, individual and pair work.*
🕐 *At least one hour.*

Previous skills/knowledge needed

Children need to be aware that the spoken and written forms of English differ from each other. They should also have some appreciation of the fact that English is spoken differently in different parts of the country and the world.

Key background information

Children may be confused about the kinds of language which are appropriate in writing and in speech. In this activity they will look at examples of dialect and will attempt to rewrite it in standard English. The following definitions may be useful.
Standard English: the variety or dialect of English which is generally used by educated people throughout the country in formal situations, especially in writing.
Dialect: a variety of English distinguished by its own characteristic features of vocabulary and grammar, spoken in a particular geographical region.

Preparation

Read through the dialect and standard English versions of the extract entitled 'Yorkshire farm labourers' on photocopiable page 137. The extract is from a conversation between two Yorkshire labourers, R.M. and A.M., in their fifties and is taken from *The LINC Reader,* edited by Ron Carter (Hodder and Stoughton, 1990). Think about the differences and similarities between the two versions. If possible, record a dialect reading of the extract on to tape. Make copies of photocopiable page 137 and cut each sheet in half so that the dialect version and the standard English version are on separate A5 pages. You will need both of the

WRITING

A5 photocopied pages for each child or pair taking part in the main activity. Then prepare the extracts needed for the extension activity on plain A5 sheets (see 'Suggestions for extension').

Resources needed
Cassette player, blank cassettes, photocopiable page 137, A4 paper, A5 paper, magazine and newspaper pictures for extension activity, pens, pencils, scissors.

What to do
Explain to the children the differences between dialect and standard English. Introduce the dialect tape and play it to them. How much did they understand? Ask them to listen carefully while the tape is played again. This time, they must

try to jot down words they think they understand. Play the tape two or three times over and then, working together as a whole group, invite the children to compare notes and to see if, between them, they have managed to write down all the words which were spoken.

Give out the A5 sheets that are the top half of photocopiable page 137 so that the children can see the transcript of the dialect extract. Explain that the words have been written *phonetically* in order to bring out the speakers' pronunciation. Does it make things easier to see the words written down like this? Working either singly or in pairs, ask the children to try to translate the dialect transcript into standard English. Give the children time to compare notes with a partner.

When the pairs have agreed on their standard English version of the transcript, invite them to rehearse a presentation of it. Allow several pairs to show their work and invite the whole class to compare versions. Lead a whole-class discussion using the following prompt questions:
▲ Which of the presentations seemed most true to the spirit of the original? Why?
▲ Do the standard English versions sound 'as good' as the dialect version? If they do not, what might be the reason?

Finally, give out A5 copies of the bottom half of photocopiable page 137, the standard English version. Use this opportunity to go over again the main issues which emerged in the earlier discussions. Points you may wish to introduce now could include:
▲ the grammatical regularity of the dialect version;
▲ the retention of old forms of the standard dialect such as 'tha' for 'thou' (second person singular);
▲ The use of figurative language such as 'dolled up' and 'walkin'' out'.

Suggestion(s) for extension
Bring in a collection of magazine and newspaper pictures showing people from different social groups – manual and 'white collar' workers, unemployed people (like labourer A.M. in the extract on photocopiable page 137), millionaires, celebrities and so on. Divide the children into pairs. Give one of each pair labourer R.M.'s extract. Give the other child in each pair labourer A.M.'s extract. The R.M. extract will be written out as dialect. The A.M. extract will be written out as standard English (copied from the version supplied for the main activity on photocopiable page 137).

The child working with the R.M. extract must find a picture which he or she thinks would fit a speaker of the dialect version. The child working with the A.M. extract must find a picture which he or she thinks would fit a speaker of the standard English version. When they have found a suitable image, each member of the pair sticks their chosen picture on to one side of a sheet of A4 paper which has been divided down the middle. Each child draws a 'speech bubble' coming out of the mouth of his or her chosen 'person' and writes either the dialect or standard English version of the extract in the bubble. On the other side, each child writes a short paragraph explaining their choice of picture.

Draw the activity to a close by inviting individual children to read out what they have written and then using their comments to lead a whole-class discussion of the relationship between dialect, standard English and social prestige.

Assessment opportunities
The activity should allow you to assess the extent to which children are able to differentiate between spoken and written forms of English. Look for evidence that they appreciate such differences.

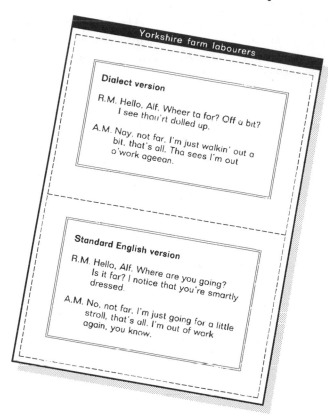

Yorkshire farm labourers

Dialect version

R.M. Hello, Alf. Wheer ta for? Off a bit? I see thou'rt dolled up.

A.M. Nay, not far. I'm just walkin' out a bit, that's all. Tha sees I'm out o'work ageean.

Standard English version

R.M. Hello, Alf. Where are you going? Is it far? I notice that you're smartly dressed.

A.M. No, not far, I'm just going for a little stroll, that's all. I'm out of work again, you know.

DIALECT AND STANDARD ENGLISH: 2

To understand how written standard English often differs from spoken dialect.

†† *Whole class, small groups.*

⏲ *At least one hour.*

Previous skills/knowledge needed
Children should appreciate that standard and dialect forms of English are different from each other. They should also have some experience of using information texts such as dictionaries.

Key background information
The main dialects spoken in England and lowland Scotland today stem from the four main dialects of Middle English: Northern, East Midland, West Midland and Southern. These dialects in their turn were influenced by other European languages such as Latin, French, Scandinavian and German.

Preparation
Enlist the support of members of staff and parent helpers willing to take part in the dialect project and brief them on what they have to do.

Resources needed
Copies of a blank map of the British Isles, A4 paper, scrap paper, pens, pencils, chalkboard. For support activity – cassette player, blank cassettes, drawing materials.

Opportunities for IT
The children could use a multimedia authoring package to create a visual and aural presentation of different dialect words. This could be set up so that when the user clicks on a dialect word it is spoken back in both dialect and standard English. The spoken words can be recorded and saved using a microphone linked to the computer and appropriate software. Other linked pages can give a textual explanation of the word, or even a map showing where the dialect word is used.

Display ideas
Look through newspapers and magazines for articles, features and advertisements which explore issues relating to standard English and dialect or which make use of dialect words and phrases to achieve their effect. Make a display of these for the classroom wall, adding labelled comments of your own which draw the children's attention to the major issues.

Other aspects of the English PoS covered
Speaking and listening – 1a, b, d; 2b; 3a, b.
Reading – 1b, c; 2a, c; 3.

Reference to photocopiable sheet
Photocopiable page 137 contains an extract from *The LINC Reader:* a dialect version of a conversation between two Yorkshire labourers and an accompanying standard English version. The children use both versions (on separate pieces of paper) in the main activity.

WRITING

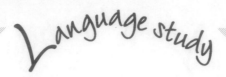

What to do

Remind the children that dialect and standard forms of English are different. Write the following list of dialect words on the board and ask the children to write down what they think the meaning of each dialect word is. You can then tell them the answers.

Dialect	Standard English
Laik	Play
Tabs	Ears
Messages	Errands
Bairns	Babies
Owt	Anything
Nowt	Nothing
Mardy	Sulky

Next invite the children to jot down on scrap paper as many words as they can think of meaning 'truce!' in a playground game of tig. Truce terms used in Great Britain include:

'keys' – Scotland
'barley' – Scotland, Wales, North-west England
'kings' – Yorkshire, Lincolnshire
'fainites' – Cornwall, Devon, Kent
'skinch' – North-east England
(from *The Lore and Language of Schoolchildren* by Iona and Peter Opie – Oxford University Press, 1987).

Let the children compare their answers.

Organise the class into teams (three or four per group). Give each group a blank map of the British Isles. In turn, let each team interview one of the members of staff/parent helpers who have volunteered to take part in the activity. The task of the interviewers is to find out what part of the country the interviewee comes from and to make a list of important dialect words he or she remembers hearing or using as a child. (If some of the interviewees have moved to Britain from another part of the English-speaking world, so much the better.)

Having collected this information, the children write the part of the country their interviewee came from on the map, drawing a line to show a rough outline of the dialect area. On a separate sheet of paper, ask the children to write the name of their interviewee and the dialect words which the interviewee has given them. The whole class then comes together and, working from their interview notes and the information compiled on the maps, each group reports back on their findings.

Suggestion(s) for extension

Ask the children to compile a glossary of dialect words and their standard English equivalents, drawing on the information gleaned from the interviews conducted at school and from discussion with family members and friends at home. Using the glossaries they have compiled, the children could rewrite a popular fairy story or nursery rhyme using as many dialect words as they can.

Suggestion(s) for support

Children could tape the interviews rather than make written notes from what they are told. You could give them a specific list of dialect words to find (agreed beforehand with the interviewee). Rather than being asked to create a glossary, less able writers might be invited to design a poster illustrating a dialect phrase collected during the interview.

Assessment opportunities

The 'reports' the children give on the interviews will provide opportunities for assessing their abilities to take notes and to shape the information collected into presentable form. Look for evidence that children appreciate the differences between spoken and written forms of English and are able to articulate their knowledge both orally and in writing.

Opportunities for IT

The children could use a word processor to create a glossary of dialect words which could be displayed in the classroom.

Display ideas

Maps, posters, glossaries and dialect stories could be displayed around the school, together with a world map showing the global influences upon the English language. This display would fit in well with a history topic such as 'The Vikings' or with a 'European Awareness' project.

Other aspects of the English PoS covered

Speaking and listening – 1a, b, c; 2a, b; 3a, b.
Reading – 1b; 2c; 3.

WRITING

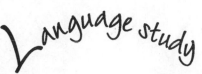

APOSTROPHES FOR ABBREVIATION

To use apostrophes for abbreviation accurately.
†† *Whole class or selected group, working independently.*
🕐 *45 minutes.*

Previous skills/knowledge needed

This activity is best undertaken when children have become aware of apostrophes and have begun to include them in their writing.

Key background information

Apostrophes can be used to show that words have been abbreviated. This is known as elision and is most commonly used when speech is reported. It is often argued that, unless abbreviated words appear within speech marks, the shortened form should not be used in writing. However, it is increasingly common for authors to use elision.

The apostrophe should denote that a letter or letters are missing. Children seem to reach a stage, usually early in Key Stage 2, when they begin to use apostrophes in what appears to be a fairly random way. This is probably the best time to explain their correct usage.

Preparation

Prepare a piece of writing which includes examples of apostrophes being used to abbreviate words. Make copies of photocopiable page 138, one for each child.

Resources needed

An example of the use of apostrophes (see above), photocopiable page 138, writing materials, chalkboard.

What to do

Show the children a piece of writing which includes words abbreviated with apostrophes and ask them to suggest what the expanded versions of the words are.

Show the children examples of elision on the board and ask them to tell you what the full forms of the words are. At this stage it is best to stick to words such as 'wouldn't', 'don't', and 'isn't' rather than discussing irregulars such as 'won't' and 'shan't'. Ask them if they know when we should use the full versions and when we should abbreviate the words. Make sure that they realise that the apostrophes are placed in the spaces where letters are missing. A common fault is the inclusion of an apostrophe in the wrong place.

Give out the copies of photocopiable page 138 and explain that in the passage on the sheet you would like them to change the abbreviated words to their fuller versions. Work through some examples to ensure that they know what is required.

As the children work, stop them occasionally to discuss common problems and to show examples of good work.

Suggestion(s) for extension

Provide another passage for the children to abbreviate words. Discuss the use of apostrophes in abbreviations of place-names on road signs and in football league tables, such as 'Middlesboro' for 'Middlesborough'.

Ask the children to look through reading books and make collections of abbreviated words.

Suggestion(s) for support

Provide children who struggle with the use of apostrophes with word lists to refer to. These might include the most common abbreviations such as 'can't', 'don't' and 'I'm'.

Assessment opportunities

Look for evidence that children can apply their knowledge of the use of apostrophes to examples which are not included on the worksheet.

Display ideas

A display of abbreviated words and their expanded forms may act as a useful reference point for the children.

Other aspects of the English PoS covered

Reading – 3.

Reference to photocopiable sheet

Photocopiable page 138 provides a passage which has several examples of words abbreviated by the use of apostrophes. The children write the full versions of the words above the abbreviated ones.

WRITING

APOSTROPHES FOR POSSESSION

To use apostrophes to show possession accurately.
†† *Whole class or selected group, working independently.*
🕐 *45 minutes.*

Key background information
This activity is intended to develop children's awareness of the correct usage of apostrophes to mark possession. The misplacing of the possessive apostrophe is probably one of the commonest errors in written English. It is not difficult to find signs in shops, or advertisements in the local press, with mistakes.

The apostrophe in possession does act as a means of abbreviation, in that it derives from Old English in which people would say 'John his house' rather than 'John's house' or 'The Smiths their family' rather than 'The Smiths' family'. It may be worth explaining this to the children. Apostrophes are placed after the name of the person or persons who own something. For example, if Emily has a bike it will be 'Emily's bike'. If a girl has socks they will be 'the girl's socks'. However, if lots of girls have socks they will be 'the girls' socks'. The apostrophe is placed after the 's' in regular plurals. This can lead to confusion when plurals are irregular

(not made by adding an 's'). Many people misplace the apostrophe in children's. It is placed before the 's' because the plural of child is children and not childrens. Further confusion often arises when using 'its'. This word only has an apostrophe when it is the shortened version of 'it is' and it should not have one when it shows possession.

Preparation
Make a collection of words which include apostrophes to mark possession. Write each word on a small piece of card and put Blu-Tack on the back of each one. Make copies of photocopiable pages 139 and 140, one of each per child.

Resources needed
Collection of examples of apostrophes marking possession (see above), children's reading books, photocopiable pages 139 and 140, writing materials, Blu-Tack, chalkboard.

What to do
Ask the children to look at the examples which you have provided and then to put the words into sentences. The children can stick the words on the board and write a sentence around each one. Talk to the children about what is meant by possession and explain that they are going to try to find some examples. Use copies of photocopiable page 139 to show the children examples of the use of apostrophes for possession.

Tell the children that they are going to skim through their reading books to find as many examples of apostrophes used to show possession as possible. Make use of their collections and write some examples on the board. Ask them if they can use the examples to make up their own sentences. They could write a short story, or part of a story, which includes examples of such words.

The exercise on photocopiable page 140 can be used to reinforce learning of the use of apostrophes for possession, or to assess children's understanding. The answers are as follows:

> Matthew's dog was stuck in the mud.
> Sarah's mother was waiting for her at the school gates.
> The boy's shoe was lost.
> The boys' toilets were locked.
> The birds' nests were high in the trees.
> Mr Dawson's car was brand new.
> Carrots, cabbages and potatoes were Nick's favourite vegetables.
> The teacher's jacket was hanging on a coat hanger.
> The teachers' classrooms were their pride and joy.
> Rovers' goal was one of the best City's goalkeeper had ever seen.
> Bills came through Bill's letter-box every day.
> The soggy tomato's skin was wrinkled.
> The potatoes' skins were burnt and black.

WRITING

Suggestion(s) for extension
Ask the children to look for examples of the use of apostrophes in shops and newspapers. They could be asked to find examples of their misuse too. Greengrocers' shops are often a particularly rich source.

Suggestion(s) for support
Children who experience difficulty should work on simple examples in which the apostrophes are applied to singular nouns and should not move on to more complex plurals until they have understood these.

Assessment opportunities
Look for signs that children are able to use apostrophes correctly in their writing, subsequent to their having completed this activity.

Other aspects of the English PoS covered
Reading – 3.

Reference to photocopiable sheets
Photocopiable page 139 provides examples of the correct use of apostrophes for children to use as a reference. Photocopiable page 140 has sentences in which the children place apostrophes.

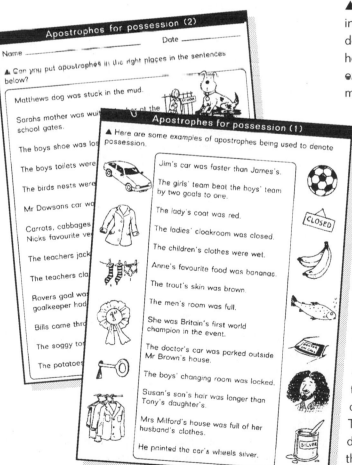

CLAUSES AND PHRASES

To understand that complex sentences are divided into clauses and phrases.

†† *Whole class, working individually.*

🕓 *At least one hour.*

Previous skills/knowledge needed
Children need to understand that written English is organised into *simple* and *complex* sentences which can be punctuated by full stops, commas, question marks and exclamation marks. They should understand the concepts of *subject* and *object* and the function they perform in sentence construction.

It would be helpful if children could also recognise the following parts of speech: noun, pronoun, adjective, verb, adverb, preposition, conjunction.

Key background information
Sentences can be divided into the following:
▲ independent main clauses – groups of words which express the main idea in a sentence.
(Joshua went home.)
▲ dependent clauses – groups of words which add extra information about the subject in the independent main clause.
(Joshua went home *because he was tired*.)
▲ phrases – a word or group of words which adds further information about the independent main clause or the dependent clause. Phrases either have no verb at all or they have a verb in the form of a *present* or *past participle*, for example 'laughing, laughed', (If you feel that the children may have difficulty with the terms *present* and *past participle*, refer to them also as 'ing' and 'ed' words.)
(*Yawning*, Joshua went home because he was tired.)

Introducing children to clause analysis can help them to understand more clearly how sentences work. This can increase their reading comprehension and help them to write with greater accuracy, precision and imagination.

Preparation
Each of the three sections of the exemplar sentence above should be written out on different coloured pieces of sugar paper and attached to a large background sheet of paper suitable for display. Draw the independent main clause in the shape of a railway engine and the dependent clause and the phrase in the shape of railway carriages. If you wish to use this activity as an opportunity to discuss conjunctions with your pupils, attach the word 'because' to a separate piece of paper and draw it in the shape of a coupling used to connect railway carriages to each other. Then you will need to prepare a second phrase and dependent clause 'carriage'. The phrase is 'Frightened', and the dependent clause is 'because he had seen something horrible'.

WRITING

Resources needed

Prepared sentence using sugar paper and large background sheet of paper (see above), writing and drawing materials. Card and word processor (optional) for support activity.

What to do

Display the large background sheet of paper so that all the children can see it. Explain that a sentence is like a train: it can be divided into parts (called *clauses*) just as a train is made up of an engine and carriages. Attach the sheet of coloured paper that has the words 'Joshua went home' and use this example to explain the meaning and purpose of the term *independent main clause*. The independent main clause is the 'engine' which 'drives' the 'sentence train'. Add the other two sheets in sequence, explaining the terms *dependent clause* and *phrase*. These are the 'carriages' of the 'sentence train': they are loaded with information which could not be delivered if the 'engine' were not there. The dependent clause and the phrase add interest and information to the original statement. Draw the children's attention to the use of the comma after 'Yawning' and explain that commas can be used to mark off one clause from another. Compare this comma to the use of the conjunction 'because' and explain how the conjunction *joins* rather than separates clauses.

Leave only the words 'Joshua went home' on the display sheet. Explain to the children that we can alter the entire meaning of the 'sentence train' by changing the 'carriages'. Discuss with the children what happens when you add the

piece of paper containing the phrase 'Frightened' to the independent main clause. Now add the dependent clause 'because he had seen something horrible'. Again, discuss the impact which the addition of this dependent clause has upon the sentence.

Ask the children to copy down the main independent clause 'Joshua went home'. Using the same sequence as before (phrase, main independent clause, dependent clause), they must now add one phrase (consisting of either an 'ing' or an 'ed' word) and one dependent clause to the sentence, so that it reads like the opening of each of the following short-story types:

▲ a love story;
▲ a cops-and-robbers story;
▲ a mystery;
▲ a funny story;
▲ a ghost story.

Invite individual children to read out their favourite lines and ask the rest of the class to guess what the chosen story style is. Which particular words give the most clues? Why?

Suggestion(s) for extension

Children could go on to work in pairs, giving each other examples of main independent clauses and examples of story types to use in building sentences. They might go on to write opening paragraphs for the stories.

Suggestion(s) for support

Slower learners might be given a selection of phrases and dependent clauses written on card in the five chosen styles. Their task could be either to match the appropriate phrases and dependent clauses to the story type, or to choose the most effective phrases and clauses from a wider selection. (It would be particularly helpful if you could prepare this material on a word processor.)

Assessment opportunities

You can test how well the children have grasped the concepts by analysing their responses in the class teaching and discussion sequences and by appraising the sentences which the children produce.

Opportunities for IT

The children could use a word-processed file which you have prepared, containing a selection of phrases and dependent and independent clauses. They could then use the 'cut and paste' or 'drag and drop' facilities to position the appropriate clauses into a single sentence.

Display ideas

The children could take one of their chosen sentences and divide it into its three sections for display purposes, just as you did for the main activity. Can they think of alternatives to the train analogy? Flowers? Outstretched hands? Mathematical symbols? Examples drawn from the same story type (a ghost story, for example) could be placed together on one poster or classroom wall to illustrate the concept of genre.

Other aspects of the English PoS covered
Speaking and listening – 1a, b, c, d; 2a, b; 3b.
Reading – 1c; 3.

NONSENSE SENTENCES

To show understanding of the principal parts of speech.

†† *Pairs.*

🕐 *One hour.*

Key background information
This activity is intended to develop children's knowledge of the main parts of speech and encourage them to look closely at sentence structure and replicate it.

Preparation
Read poems by Edward Lear, James Reeves and Spike Milligan to show the children how poets can write apparent nonsense which entertains the reader. These can be found in Edward Lear's *Non-sense* (Rizzoli International Publications, Inc. 1994), *Complete Poems for Children* by James Reeves (Heinemann, 1994) and Spike Milligan's *Silly Verse for Kids* (Penguin, 1970). Other books which contain nonsense poems are *The Faber Book of Nursery Verse* edited by Barbara Ireson (Faber & Faber, 1983) and *The Quentin Blake Book of Nonsense Verse* (Viking, 1994). Make copies of photocopiable page 141, one for each pair.

Resources needed
Samples of nonsense poems (see above), photocopiable page 141, writing materials, chalkboard.

What to do
Provide examples of nonsense sentences on the board and discuss them. The following may be useful:

> The blue dog drove carefully along the slow book.
> The cold grass clapped softly in the big button.
> The yellow rain drew stupidly on the old sky.

Ask the children if they can make one up with your help, using the same pattern as in your sentences. Encourage them to discuss the structure of the sentence and the role of each of the words. If they are familiar with terms such as adjective, noun, verb and adverb, use them. If not they could be introduced or reintroduced at this stage.

After introducing the idea of nonsense sentences, tell the children that they will be writing their own. Give out copies of photocopiable page 141 which has examples and tell them that they must follow the same pattern when they write. Insist that they do not write anything which could be described as sensible! Initially, the activity is best done in pairs so that children can discuss sentence structure and parts of speech.

Suggestion(s) for extension
If the children are doing well they may go on to produce sentences individually. These may be linked together to form poems or pieces of humorous prose.

Suggestion(s) for support
Some children may be given simple sentences which contain only one noun, one verb and an adjective at first. As they become more familiar with the task, they may move on to more complex sentences.

Assessment opportunities
Throughout the activity note which children are able to identify adjectives, nouns, verbs, adverbs, definite and indefinite articles.

Opportunities for IT
The children could do their writing using a word processor so that the sentences they create can easily be edited or words in the sentences can be moved to new positions.

Display ideas
Sentences and pieces of poetry or prose may be displayed, together with appropriate pictures.

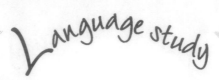

Other aspects of the English PoS covered
Reading – 3.
Speaking and listening – 3b.

Reference to photocopiable sheet
Photocopiable page 141 provides three groups of nonsense sentences of increasing complexity.

USE OF ADJECTIVES

To use adjectives effectively to enhance writing.
†† *Whole class or group, working individually.*
🕘 *50–60 minutes.*

Key background information
This activity is intended to show children how adjectives may be used to enliven their writing and make it more interesting to read. They will also examine the ways in which authors make use of adjectives in published texts.

Preparation
Find examples of texts in which authors have used adjectives imaginatively. Make copies of photocopiable pages 142 and 143.

Resources needed
Poems and passages of prose (see above), photocopiable pages 142 and 143, dictionaries, thesauruses, chalkboard, writing materials.

What to do
Read a piece of poetry or prose to the children and ask them questions about the appearance of characters and so forth. Elicit from them that it is the adjectives which enable us to know more about the way things look, feel, taste or smell. Point to things around the classroom and ask the children to provide adjectives which would describe them.

Provide sentences on the board which contain no adjectives. For example, 'The boy hit the ball with a bat.' Ask the children to bring the sentence to life by adding adjectives to describe the boy, the ball and the bat. Repeat the exercise until the children are confident about using adjectives.

Now give out copies of photocopiable pages 142 and 143. The two sheets are designed to allow for differentiation by reading ability (it may be necessary to produce extra sheets depending upon the ability range within the class). The sheets contain passages which have no adjectives and the children's task is to add adjectives to make the passage more interesting. It should be emphasised to the children that there are no correct answers and that they may choose any words which they feel are appropriate. Dictionaries should be used to aid spelling and to provide ideas, and additional ideas could be sought in thesauruses. Rather than copying the passage out, the children should write in additional words using arrows. They may go on to continue the passage by writing a further paragraph which includes interesting adjectives.

When the children have finished the work, they should read out their efforts and compare their ideas with others. Childen who finish early could devise their own bland passages for others to work on.

Suggestion(s) for extension
Children who grasp the idea of adjectives easily may attempt to add adverbs to the passage. Children could go on to write their own descriptive work including adjectives and adverbs where appropriate. This work might be used as a prelude to creative writing.

Suggestion(s) for support
Children who find the activity difficult can be supplied with some sample adjectives to help them, or they might do the exercise orally before attempting writing.

Assessment opportunities
Look for examples of children making good choices of vocabulary and note their understanding of the term adjective.

Opportunities for IT
A set of sentences without adjectives, tailored to the abilities of the children, could be prepared using a word processor. The children could then add adjectives, highlighting them with a different font. They could use an electronic thesaurus to search for appropriate and interesting adjectives to use.

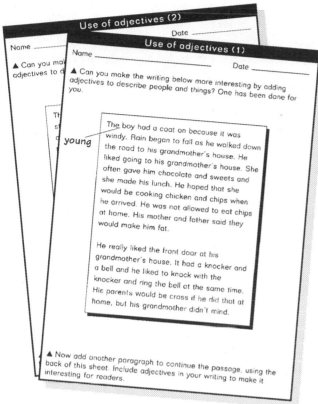

Use of adjectives (2)

Name _____ Date _____

Use of adjectives (1)

Name _____ Date _____

▲ Can you make the writing below more interesting by adding adjectives to describe people and things? One has been done for you.

young

The boy had a coat on because it was windy. Rain began to fall as he walked down the road to his grandmother's house. He liked going to his grandmother's house. She often gave him chocolate and sweets and she made his lunch. He hoped that she would be cooking chicken and chips when he arrived. He was not allowed to eat chips at home. His mother and father said they would make him fat.

He really liked the front door at his grandmother's house. It had a knocker and a bell and he liked to knock with the knocker and ring the bell at the same time. His parents would be cross if he did that at home, but his grandmother didn't mind.

▲ Now add another paragraph to continue the passage, using the back of this sheet. Include adjectives in your writing to make it interesting for readers.

Display ideas
The word-processed sentences in which the children have incorporated adjectives could be displayed under a heading 'Adjectives add meaning'.

Other aspects of the English PoS covered
Reading – 3.

Reference to photocopiable sheets
Photocopiable pages 142 and 143 provide examples of writing which lack adjectives. You can use the sheets according to the range of reading ability within your class. Photocopiable page 143 is for a more advanced stage of reading than photocopiable page 142.

SIMILES

To understand and make use of similes.

†† *Whole class, pairs and individuals.*

🕐 *At least one hour.*

Previous skills/knowledge required
Children should show some awareness of the ways in which the authors of their favourite poems and stories have used language to excite and engage the reader.

Key background information
A simile is a part of speech in which one thing is compared to another by the words 'like' or 'as': for example, 'as bright as a button'.

Preparation
Choose a favourite short poem or prose extract which paints effective word-pictures through the use of similes. Ask the children to bring to the lesson a piece of writing by one of their favourite authors. Explain that it must be one which paints a vivid picture in words. Have a selection of poetry anthologies on hand for the children to browse through in case anyone is stuck for ideas in the shared reading section of the lesson. Prepare one copy per child of the exercise on photocopiable page 144. Study the information on the extracts given in 'What to do'.

Resources needed
A copy of your chosen extract, a selection of poetry anthologies (see above), photocopiable page 144, writing materials. Potato crisps for extension activity.

What to do
Introduce and read your chosen poem or prose extract to the children, explaining to them why the author's use of figurative language (including similes) has made it so memorable for you. Tell the children what the word 'simile' means and give them an example from your chosen passage. Now invite the children to read their favourite poem or prose extract to a partner (five minutes for each person). Can they identify effective uses of figurative language (including

'like a knife-blade slicing the sky in two'

Suggestion(s) for extension

Remind the children that effective similes help us to look at familiar things in new and interesting ways. Distribute some crisps, one or two per child. Ask the children to imagine they were describing a crisp to somebody who had never seen or tasted one before. The children must write a 'simile list' for their crisp, finding effective images to describe its colour, smell, shape, taste, and appearance. Each line must contain the word 'like' or 'as'. When the list is complete, the children should add a commentary, explaining why they chose those particular images.

Suggestion(s) for support

All of these activities (including the introductory reading) could be carried out in pairs or small groups rather than individually. Some children may need the support of a list of sample similes and might be asked to comment orally rather than in writing on their choices.

Assessment opportunities

The reading activity provides an opportunity to assess the children's abilities to express opinions and preferences about their choice of writing. Children's grasp of the concept of similes can be assessed through their choice of images and, particularly, through their commentary upon that choice. The exercise on photocopiable page 144 also offers opportunities for the assessment of pupils' grasp of syntax.

Opportunities for IT

The children could use a word processor to experiment with different words to use in their similes before committing themselves to a choice of words.

similes)? Invite one or two children to read out their passages and then, as a whole class, share ideas about the ways in which writers can paint effective pictures in words.

Distribute the copies of photocopiable page 144. Explain that each of the extracts is taken from a poem and that poets are particularly good at using similes to help us see things in a new way.

Extract 1 is taken from the poem 'Sleeping Cats' by Moira Andrew in *Poetry – Scholastic Collections* (Scholastic Ltd, 1992). The cats who 'dedicate their lives to dozing' are 'stretched out like pulled gum before the gas fire'.

Extract 2 is taken from the poem 'For F.E.H.' by Frances Horovitz in *Collected Poems* (Bloodaxe, 1985). An old man is stretched out on a bed, dying. He is so thin and emaciated that she describes him as being 'weightless as shaved bone'.

Extract 3 is taken from the poem 'Aeroplane' by Celia Warren in *Poetry – Scholastic Collections* (Scholastic Ltd, 1992). The poet describes the trail of vapour from the aeroplane as being 'like a knife-blade slicing the sky in two'.

Extract 4 is taken from the poem 'A Gift from the Stars' by John Rice (unpublished), describing the King and Queen of Christmas who travel high above the clouds where 'the silent comets run'. Their eyes are 'like far mountains' and their robes 'flow like soft stream water'.

Invite the children to supply their own similes, adding a sentence explaining why they made that particular choice. When they have finished the exercise take the children through the extracts, asking them to offer possible answers for the missing text before showing them what the poet wrote. Ask the children to write a short response to this information, saying whether or not they preferred the poet's simile to their own and why.

Similes: painting pictures in words

Name _____

Date _____

▲ Poets are especially good at using similes to paint pictures in words. Read these four extracts and listen carefully to what your teacher tells you about them. Can you write imaginative words to make the similes complete?

From *Sleeping Cats* by Moira Andrew

Cats dedicate their lives to dozing.

Stretched out like _____

From *For F.E.H.* by Frances Horovitz

The old man stretched on his bed, weightless as _____

_____

From *Aeroplane* by Celia Warren

Like a _____

a vapour cuts cleanly through the blue;

the only white in a cloudless day

From *Gift from the Stars* by John Rice

Their eyes are distant and blue, like _____

Their silky robes flow like _____

▲ When you have finished, can you say why you chose the words you did? Write a sentence for each of the four extracts.

▲ When your teacher tells you the words that the poets used, can you say which you prefer – your similes or theirs? Write a sentence for each of the four extracts.

WRITING

Display ideas
Collect pictures from newspapers and magazines which suit the images chosen by the children for the cloze, simile list and poetry writing activities. Use this material to mount a display called 'Similes: painting pictures in words'.

Other aspects of the English PoS covered
Speaking and listening – 1a; 2a; 3b.
Reading – 1a, c, d; 2b, c.

Reference to photocopiable sheet
Photocopiable page 144 provides four extracts from poems to enable the children to insert their own similes and write about their choices.

ONOMATOPOEIA
To understand and use onomatopoeic words in writing.
†† *Whole class, working individually.*
🕐 *One hour.*

Previous skills/knowledge needed
Children need to have worked on descriptive prose and poetry.

Key background information
Onomatopoeic words imitate the sound of the thing they describe, for example 'crunch', 'squelch', 'hiss', 'swish', 'slurp' and 'splash'. This activity is intended to help children to develop their imaginative writing through consideration of vocabulary choices.

Preparation
It would be a good idea to use a movement lesson to encourage the use of movement fitted to onomatopoeic words. Spike Milligan's 'The Ning Nang Nong' which appears in *Silly Verse for Kids* in *Mini Milligan Collection* (Puffin, 1992) is a simple example of the use of onomatopoeia which you could read to the children. Prepare a list of onomatopoeic words on the board. Make copies of photocopiable page 145. You will need one for each child.

Resources needed
A selection of onomatopoeic words, examples of poems which use onomatopoeia such as 'The Ning Nang Nong' (see above), photocopiable page 145, writing materials, chalkboard.

What to do
Write the word 'onomatopoeia' on the board and explain what it means. Show the children some examples of onomatopoeic words and see if they can make lists of others, either in groups or as a class. Talk with the children about a selection of onomatopoeic words which you have written on the board. Ask them what is special about the words. If they find it difficult to answer try acting some of the words.

Give each child a copy of photocopiable page 145 and ask the children to complete the cloze exercise on the photocopiable sheet using onomatopoeic words. Tell them that there are no correct answers, but that you are looking for imaginative onomatopoeic words. Discuss what they have done.

When they have finished, ask them to write their own piece of descriptive writing and include within it as many onomatopoeic words as they can. It will be helpful to read some examples of poems which use this device. If the

weather is wet children could go for a short walk in the playground and consider the sounds which they hear. Alternatively, a selection of items which could be used to make noises could be provided. For example, dried leaves, boxes of dried peas, squeezable paint bottles and straws in tumblers of water could be used to encourage children to consider vocabulary choices. Children can be asked to invent their own onomatopoeic words to describe the sounds.

Suggestion(s) for extension
Draw the children's attention to a class list of onomatopoeic words and encourage them to add to it whenever they find such words in their reading.

WRITING

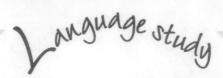

Onomatopoeia

Name _____ Date _____

▲ Can you fill in the spaces using onomatopoeic words?

Oliver hurried down the stairs and ran towards the kitchen. He was afraid.

He had heard a loud _____ from the room and he wondered what

had happened.

As he walked into the kitchen he saw his sister drop a plate. It went

_____ on the floor. 'Oh no, that's another one!' said Hannah.

'Every time I wash up I seem to _____ the crockery.'

Oliver went to the sink to help, but another plate dropped into the water

with a _____. He felt the bits of broken plate _____ under

his shoes as he walked to the cupboard to fetch a dustpan and brush.

His sister let the water out of the sink and Oliver heard it _____

down the plug hole. The floor was wet and messy. 'Let's have a drink,' said

Hannah. She put orange squash into two glasses and turned on the tap.

The water _____ out of the tap and _____ into the glasses.

'It's almost as wet in here as it is outside,' said Oliver. Outside the wind

_____ and the rain _____ on to the pavement.

'Let's clear up before Mum and Dad find us,' whispered Hannah. 'I think

I heard a door _____ing upstairs.'

Suggestion(s) for support

Children who experience difficulties may work with a partner or an adult scribe. They might be provided with a selection of onomatopoeic words to help them with vocabulary choice and spelling.

Assessment opportunities

Look for evidence that children are making informed attempts to spell words using their phonic knowledge. Look for imaginative use of vocabulary.

Opportunities for IT

Children could use a drawing package to enter their words and alter them, stretching or bending the words into expressive shapes. The children could experiment with the talking facilities of some word processors to try to obtain appropriate sounds. This may mean adding extra consonants and vowels to the original spelling.

Display ideas

Next to a display of the children's onomatopoeic writing, display items which children can use to make noises with. Invite them to visit the display and write on a displayed piece of paper their ideas for appropriate onomatopoeic words.

Other aspects of the English PoS covered

Reading – 2b.

Reference to photocopiable sheet

Photocopiable page 145 provides a passage with missing words. The children should use onomatopoeic words to fill in the spaces.

PRÉCIS

To demonstrate an ability to edit and to write concisely.

†† *Whole class or group.*

⏱ *One hour.*

Key background information

The children will discover in this activity that ideas which are expressed in a detailed and elaborate way sometimes need to be written concisely.

The activity may be best suited to the most able children in a Year 5 or Year 6 class initially, but it may then be developed for a broader ability range.

Preparation

Make enough copies of photocopiable page 146 so that you have one for each child.

Resources needed

Photocopiable page 146, writing materials.

What to do

Give the children copies of photocopiable page 146 so that they can analyse it as a class. Discuss the way in which the information can be given in different forms using different numbers of words. Ask them to decide upon the number of words which a third shorter passage should have and work with them to achieve this. Tell the children to write down their reduced version on a sheet of paper. Ask them if this final passage still contains all the information included in the first passage.

Then ask each child to choose a subject and write it at the top of a piece of paper. You may decide to choose the subject yourself. Tell them that they must write about the subject using exactly 80 words. If they find it difficult to use the exact number of words suggest that they look for unnecessary words and eliminate them. For example, they might use commas to replace 'and', or they might take out conjunctions and increase the number of sentences.

When the children have finished they should check their work to make sure that it is legible and accurate while they wait for others to finish. They should then fold down the title and pass the paper on to the next person, who has to rewrite the passage using 40 words. When this is finished the first passage is folded down so that the next writer may only see the 40-word piece. Children then rewrite the passages using 20 words. The process is repeated with children writing only ten words. At the end let children read aloud from the sheets and discuss the ways in which they managed to reduce the length of passages without eliminating information.

Suggestion(s) for extension

Children who manage the activity well could attempt to précis sections of well-known children's stories.

Suggestion(s) for support

It may be advisable to provide some children with specific topics for the writing and to have their work monitored by an adult helper so that they gradually learn how to cut out less important words.

Assessment opportunities

Note the children's abilities to consider their use of language and make vocabulary choices.

Opportunities for IT

The original text can be prepared using a word processor so that children can undertake this activity at the computer. The children could begin with a printed version so that they can work away from the computer, returning to it to manipulate the text on screen. They will need to use the full range of editing commands and it will be helpful for them to know how to use the word-count facility.

Display ideas

Display the sheets with all versions of the writing visible so that children can see how the initial passage was changed as it was reduced in length.

Other aspects of the English PoS covered

Reading – 2c.

Reference to photocopiable sheet

Photocopiable page 146 provides information written in 150 words and then reduced to 80 words. The children are asked to reduce it still further.

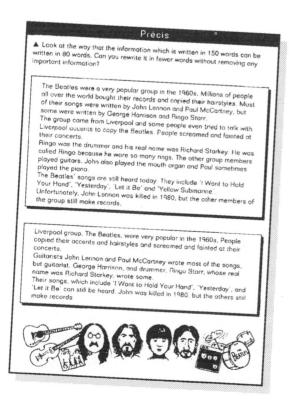

TURNING A DRAMA SCRIPT INTO PROSE

To be able to present text which has been read in one genre in a different form.

†† *Whole class or group, working individually.*

⏱ *One hour.*

Key background information

This activity is designed to encourage children to look at the devices used in drama scripts and consider carefully how they might convey the ideas in the script in an alternative form.

Preparation

Provide examples of scripts which are within the children's reading capabilities. This activity may be an ideal way of introducing children to the structure of scripts, as a prelude to their performing in a school play or class assembly. Choose excerpts which are interesting and which children can easily understand and interpret. Make copies of photocopiable page 147, one for each child.

WRITING

Resources needed

Appropriate scripts (see above), photocopiable page 147, writing materials. Overhead projector (optional).

What to do

Talk with the children about the format of the scripts. If the formats vary discuss the different ways in which they are set out. Explain that the characters do not say all of the words which are written down and tell them about stage directions and headings to denote who is speaking. Show them examples, perhaps using an overhead projector, and let them read the part of the play so that they begin to see which words should be spoken. Ask them to describe what happens in the play. It may be useful to have some children act out the script.

Show the children the script on photocopiable page 147 and explain that they are going to rewrite it in prose. Work through part of the script orally before asking the children to work independently. Stop the children occasionally so that they can share their ideas with the class and so that you can monitor the work and ensure that everyone is clear about the task.

When the majority of the class have completed the activity, read aloud or have the children read aloud the work and invite constructive comments. Children who finish early might go on to continue the story and write about what happens when the fire brigade arrives.

Turning a drama script into prose

▲ Read the script and then rewrite it in prose.

MRS SMITH	Sam, are you ready for school yet?
SAM (calling)	I can't come down, Mum.
MRS SMITH	Whatever is the matter, Sam?
SAM	I'm stuck!
MRS SMITH (running up the stairs)	What do you mean you're stuck? What have you done? (She sees Sam) Oh no!
SAM	I'm sorry, Mum. I didn't mean to do it.
MRS SMITH	You silly boy! Why did you put your toe in the tap in the first place? It can't have been an accident.
SAM (crying)	I didn't mean to, honestly. It just sort of happened.
MRS SMITH	Well, I'm going downstairs to phone the fire brigade. They'll know how to get you out. Don't go away!
SAM (shouting)	Oh please don't ring them, Mum. I don't want a lot of fireman to see me in the bath!
MRS SMITH	You should have thought of that before you got your toe stuck in the tap.

(Mrs Smith goes out of the room and picks up the telephone. She presses three times on the same button.)

| MRS SMITH | Hello... yes, fire brigade please... yes, I'll hold on. Hello, Fire Brigade? Yes, I'm sorry to bother you, but it's my son... No he hasn't lit a fire, he's got his toe stuck in the bath tap... Yes, that's what I said to him. You'll come round and see what you can do.. Oh thank you... 23 Spring Road... Right, I'll see you in a few minutes. Oh, you won't be coming yourself, your mates will... All right. Thank you very much. Goodbye. |

▲ Can you finish the story? Write in script form or in prose.

Suggestion(s) for extension

Children could rewrite stories which they had previously written, changing them into a script format.

Suggestion(s) for support

Some children may need to work with more able partners or have access to an adult scribe. Specific teaching of the punctuation of speech may be necessary before this activity is attempted.

Assessment opportunities

Look for examples of children making use of speech marks and use the assessment formatively to revise this aspect of punctuation with those children who need help. Note, too, their abilities to write in sentences.

Opportunities for IT

The drama script could be presented to children in a word-processed form which they can then alter to a prose version on screen, writing preliminary notes on paper if necessary.

Display ideas

Display photocopiable page 147 and any other examples of scripts together with the children's rewrites so that children may compare them.

Other aspects of the English PoS covered

Speaking and listening – 1d.
Reading –1a.

Reference to photocopiable sheet

Photocopiable page 147 provides a section of a drama script which children can rewrite in prose.

FORTUNATELY/ UNFORTUNATELY

To write sentences which begin with adverbs.
†† *Group or pairs.*
🕐 *One hour.*

Key background information
This activity is designed to encourage children to develop their knowledge of sentence structure and to encourage the use of adverbs. The use of adverbs to begin sentences is not common in children's writing at Key Stage 2 and this activity is intended to make children more aware of the possibilities which exist for structuring their sentences.

Preparation
Write your own 'fortunately/unfortunately' passage which is relevant to the children in your class or use the one on photocopiable page 148. You will need one copy for each pair or one per group.

Resources needed
Example of a fortunately/unfortunately passage, photocopiable page 148, writing materials, chalkboard. Cassette player and blank cassettes for the support activity.

What to do
Read the children an example of a 'fortunately/unfortunately' passage and discuss its format. Try to create another one with the children orally. Write the words 'fortunately' and 'unfortunately' on the board, as they tend to be misspelled.

When the children have understood the activity tell them that they are going to produce 'fortunately/unfortunately' passages together. At this stage give out the copies of photocopiable page 148 which the children can refer to if they need ideas. Explain that everyone will be given a piece of paper and that each person must write an interesting sentence which begins with the word 'fortunately'. After this has been done by everyone the sheets of paper are passed on and the next child adds a sentence which begins with 'unfortunately' and which is linked to the first sentence. This continues with the words 'fortunately' and 'unfortunately' being used alternately until you feel that it is a good time to stop. The writing may be passed around the group or could be passed back and forth between partners. The latter approach has the advantage that children can work at their own pace without being held up by the rest of the group. However, the writing can be less interesting because fewer people have contributed. It is a good idea to end on a positive note with a sentence beginning with 'fortunately'.

When everyone is ready have the children take turns to read one of the passages aloud to the rest of the group. If the activity has gone well it could be repeated. If children have found the activity difficult it may be a good idea to work with the group orally, using the board to produce the writing co-operatively, before the children make a second attempt.

Suggestion(s) for extension
Children could work in pairs using other pairs of words such as 'happily' and 'sadly', 'quickly' and 'slowly' , or 'sensibly' and 'stupidly'.

Suggestion(s) for support
Some children could work in pairs to produce sentences together. Sentences could be recorded on to tape and written up later with a scribe.

Assessment opportunities
Look for imaginative sentences and note children's abilities to punctuate sentences accurately.

Display ideas
Children could select a few sentences beginning with each word and write these on separate pieces of paper, displaying 'fortunately' sentences under a heading 'Fortunately' and 'unfortunately' sentences under a heading 'Unfortunately'. Children could then use the display to pair sentences.

Other aspects of the English PoS covered
Speaking and listening – 3b.

Reference to photocopiable sheet
Photocopiable page 148 provides an example of a fortunately/unfortunately story which can be used for reference.

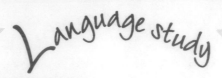

BANK ROBBERY

To write using the features of standard written English, including the use of accurate punctuation and spelling and a range of parts of speech to enhance the quality of writing.

†† *Whole class or group, working individually.*

⊕ *At least one hour.*

Previous skills/knowledge needed

This activity should be attempted when children have reached the end of the language study chapter of this book and have developed confidence in their writing.

Key background information

In this activity the children are provided with a newspaper report. They are asked to read the report and then write in greater detail about the event, imagining that they were one of the people mentioned in the article.

The activity is designed to enable you to assess a range of skills, particularly those related to language study.

Preparation

Photocopy the report on page 149 (you will need one copy for each child) and provide copies of other newspaper articles. Make copies of the assessment sheet on photocopiable page 150 for your own use.

Resources needed

Newspaper reports, photocopiable pages 149 and 150, dictionaries, writing materials.

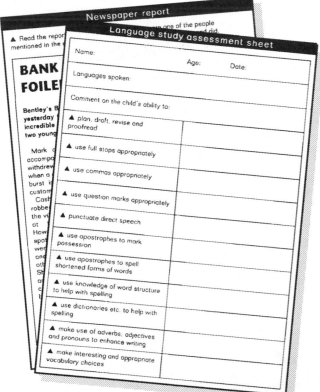

What to do

Discuss the newspaper reports with the children and read some examples. Ask them to retell the stories orally and invite them to imagine that they were present when events took place and ask them to expand upon what might have happened.

When the children are familiar with the idea of newspaper reports and understand how they could retell the stories in their own words, explain that you have a copy of another report for them to look at, and give out the copies of photocopiable page 149. This time they will be writing an account of what happened as if they were present. It might take the form of a statement for the police or it could be written as a story or a report for another newspaper.

Discuss possible audiences for the writing with the children and tell the children that you are particularly interested in seeing what they can do when they work independently. They may use dictionaries and other resources, but should do so unaided. Encourage them to proofread and revise their work before presenting a final copy.

Suggestion(s) for extension

Some children could take their reports and produce a news bulletin with different eyewitness accounts of the attempted robbery. This could be performed for the rest of the class or as part of an assembly.

Suggestion(s) for support

Some children may need to be provided with word banks or may require help with structuring their work. If help is given this should be noted when assessments are recorded.

Assessment opportunities

Look for evidence that children are able to distinguish between spoken and written language and can use appropriate punctuation and grammar. Note the extent to which they make use of adjectives, adverbs and pronouns to enhance and vary their writing, and look for signs that they are able to spell regular words accurately.

Display ideas

A display of published reports could be used to accompany a display of the children's work.

Other aspects of the English PoS covered

Speaking and listening – 1a; 2a, b.
Reading – 1a, c; 2b, c; 3.

Reference to photocopiable sheets

Photocopiable page 149 provides an example of a newspaper report for children to use as a starting point for their work. Photocopiable page 150 is a language study assessment sheet.

Persuasive writing

In this chapter extensive use is made of examples of persuasive writing which children meet in everyday life. There are opportunities to write letters, advertisements and argumentative prose.

As children get older their reading and writing is increasingly of a persuasive nature. Reading matter might range from newspaper editorials to advertisements and from political pamphlets to posters. It is important that they begin to appreciate that writing is a powerful tool for persuading people to your point of view and that they should be sceptical about believing everything which they read.

The activities in this section offer opportunities not only to study persuasive writing, but also to produce it. It is hoped that the activities will increase awareness of the importance of vocabulary choices, style and presentation in producing convincing persuasive writing.

Within the genre of persuasive writing there are many different forms of writing. Job applications, for example, require a quite different style from that needed to produce a classified ad. Similarly, guidebooks differ in tone from letters to and from a problem page. It is hoped that the activities in this section will raise awareness of the range and scope of persuasive writing.

WRITING

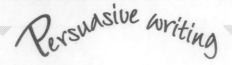

FACT OR OPINION?

To use writing persuasively.

†† *Whole class, small group and individual work.*

🕐 *At least one hour for the main activity; 45 minutes for each of the extension activities.*

Previous skills/knowledge needed

Children should have some awareness of the fact that language can be ambiguous. Jokes, riddles, puns, advertising slogans and tabloid newspaper headlines can help children appreciate that words can have more than one meaning.

Key background information

All authors have in mind an ideal reader who will respond to their writing in exactly the way they would wish. In this sense, all texts attempt to 'position' their readers. For example, the 'ideal' reader of a car advertisement would be someone who immediately went out and bought the car. Sometimes, we do not wish to respond as the author would like. When we 'resist' in this way, we are said to be 'reading against the text'.

Preparation

Duplicate photocopiable pages 151 and 152 so that you have a copy of both pages for each child.

Resources needed

Photocopiable pages 151 and 152, A4 paper, felt-tipped pens, pens, pencils. Newspapers, magazines and comics for extension activity.

What to do

Describe to the children the differences between a fact and an opinion. Give out copies of photocopiable page 151 and ask the children to read the sentences on the sheet and to decide which is a fact and which an opinion. Invite the children to give their answers and encourage them to explain which words or phrases in the sentence helped them come to their decision. Were there any which seemed part fact, part opinion? Now distribute copies of the Anytown Pleasure Park advertisement on photocopiable page 152. Ask each child to read the advertisement according to the following instructions:

▲ Underline the words and phrases which you regard as facts in one colour, and those you regard as opinions in another.

▲ Make a list of the things described in this advertisement which you would like to do. Explain your choice.

▲ Make a list of the things described in this advertisement which you would not like to do. Explain your choice.

▲ Write a few sentences describing the kind of people you think this advertisement is aimed at. (Think about their age, sex, where they might live, what they might do for a living.)

▲ Are you like the person you have just described? Would you be tempted to visit the Pleasure Park? Write a few sentences explaining your answer.

▲ Select one particular word or phrase from the advertisement which strikes you as being especially 'over the top'. Explain your choice.

The children can compare their answers in groups of three or four before coming together as a whole class to share their ideas. Finally, ask each child to write a 'letter' to the Advertising Standards Authority, pointing out the Pleasure Park advertisement's factual inaccuracies and arguing that it should not be published. They should try, when writing, to use the persuasion techniques they have observed in their analysis of the Pleasure Park advertisement.

Suggestion(s) for extension

Children could choose a real advertisement from a magazine, comic or newspaper and analyse it in the manner described above. Alternatively, they could create an advertisement designed to show the world how wonderful they are. (The children will find this particular activity easier if they are given a specific genre to parody – for example, a toy, toothpaste, washing powder or cat food commercial.)

Suggestion(s) for support

Some children may need to read through the advertisement on photocopiable page 152 with an adult and be helped to follow the instructions.

Assessment opportunities

The children's written response to the Pleasure Park advertisement and their letter to the Advertising Standards

Authority offer opportunities to assess their understanding of the ways in which language can be used to manipulate and persuade, from the point of view of both 'target audience' and 'persuader'. These two written responses will also provide opportunities to assess the children's capacity to 'read between the lines' and to understand the importance of syntax and vocabulary use.

Opportunities for IT
The children could use a word processor to write, draft and present their letter to the Advertising Standards Authority. Show children how to use the correct formatting commands to lay out the letter, rather than using the space bar to position text. This should include such features as 'right justification' for the address, a single space between paragraphs, centring for the 'Yours faithfully' line and so on.

Display ideas
The children could create a collage of their own and nationally recognised advertising images, labelling them with comments about the ways in which the advertisements use language to achieve their effects.

Other aspects of the English PoS covered
Speaking and listening – 1a, b, c, d; 2a; 3b.
Reading – 1b, c; 2b, c.

Reference to photocopiable sheets
The children decide which sentences are facts and which are opinions on photocopiable page 151. Photocopiable page 152 provides an advertisement for the children to analyse.

LABELS AND DIRECTIONS
To produce instructional writing.
†† *Whole class or group, working individually or in pairs.*
🕐 *At least one hour.*

Key background information
This activity is designed to encourage children to look at the information provided on packaged goods. Packaging of household items usually fulfils two roles: it provides information about the product, its contents and where it is produced; it attempts to persuade the consumer to buy the product by making claims about its effectiveness. In this activity the children will read and write in different forms.

Preparation
Bring to school a selection of household items (preferably empty boxes, cans and bottles) which have labels showing what the products can do and directions for use. It is important to ensure that the containers do not have toxic or otherwise dangerous materials in them.

Resources needed
Shampoo bottles, aerosol cans, washing powder boxes and so on (see above), chalkboard, writing materials.

What to do
Show the children the containers and talk about the contents. Ask them how they would know how to use the products and emphasise potential dangers. After cautioning the children about careful handling of the items, distribute them and ask the children to read the labels. Discuss the different labels and write some key words on the board.

Many products have labels which extol the virtues of the goods as well as directions for use. Discuss with the children how language differs according to purpose.

Tell the children that they are going to design their own labels for imaginary products. They will need to write a few sentences which will persuade people to buy the products, and they will also need to provide directions for use and warnings about safety.

Suggestion(s) for extension
Children might make their own collections of words which feature regularly on packaging and put them into groups of, say, persuasive words, describing words, cautionary words and instructional words. They could devise their own categories.

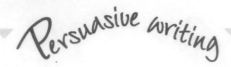
Suggestion(s) for support

Children may work in pairs for support, or with an adult helper. Some children may need to have lists of words supplied for them.

Assessment opportunities

Note evidence of children being able to adopt contrasting styles to describe the product and to provide directions for its use.

Display ideas

Display the labelled containers on a shelf with supermarket signs or include them in a class shop.

Other aspects of the English PoS covered

Reading – 2c.

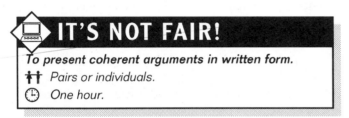

IT'S NOT FAIR!

To present coherent arguments in written form.

†† *Pairs or individuals.*

🕐 *One hour.*

Key background information

This activity is designed to draw upon children's thoughts and feelings about justice and injustice and to encourage them to write persuasively.

Preparation

Find a copy of 'It's Not Fair' by Allan Ahlberg.

Resources needed

'It's Not Fair' by Allan Ahlberg from *Please Mrs Butler* (Puffin, 1984), writing materials (including pieces of vertically folded paper). Cassette player and blank cassettes for support activity.

What to do

Read the poem 'It's Not Fair'. Ask the children if they think that the boy in the poem is right to think that so many things are unfair.

Talk with them about justice and injustice and ask them to list the things which they find unfair on one half of a piece of vertically folded paper. Next ask them or their partners to look at the list and write solutions to the problems on the adjacent half of the paper. Discuss the responses and the children's solutions.

Ask the children to select one issue about which they feel strongly and write about it. Encourage them to suggest how they would solve the problem. The issue may be related to the environment, to animal welfare, to school life or to any other area which concerns the children. Read aloud, or ask the children to read aloud, the completed pieces of work.

Suggestion(s) for extension

Children might write to local councillors or Members of Parliament, or to the headteacher about the issues. They should be encouraged to write persuasively but politely.

Suggestion(s) for support

Children could begin by tape-recording their ideas and then go on to write them with the help of a writing partner.

Assessment opportunities

Note the children's abilities to write persuasively and to produce coherent arguments.

Opportunities for IT

Children could use a word processor to write, draft and present their letter about a particular issue, possibly using a writing frame set up on the computer to help them structure their writing. This could include a number of beginnings of sentences which would encourage writing in the persuasive genre and which children would expand or add to as they need. These could include:

▲ I think that...

▲ My first reason is...

▲ A further reason is...

▲ Furthermore...

By using the framework above, the children are encouraged to state their opening position; put forward the arguments which have influenced their decision; and provide a brief summary of their viewpoint.

Display ideas

Display Ahlberg's poem at the centre of a display of writing on the subject 'It's Not Fair'.

Other aspects of the English PoS covered

Speaking and listening – 2b.

A GUIDE TO THE SCHOOL

To write for a range of audiences.

†† *Pairs or small groups.*

🕑 *An extended writing project which may be undertaken over a few days.*

Key background information

In this activity children are encouraged to write for a wide audience. They will be given the task of producing a guidebook for their school which could be shown to visitors. It is important to stress that the guidebooks will be intended to persuade people that theirs is a good school!

Preparation

This activity might follow a visit to a museum, castle or stately home where a guidebook was provided. Find examples of guidebooks to show to the children.

Resources needed

Guidebooks, paper, pencils, card, chalkboard.

What to do

Show examples of guidebooks to the children and ask them to suggest the attributes of a good guidebook. There are many guidebooks which are produced specifically for children and examples should be sought.

Having established the qualities of a good guidebook, ask the groups to brainstorm their ideas for what a school guidebook might include. Share the ideas on the board and try to establish sections which the children could include in their books. It may be a good idea to ask one child to be responsible for each section. These children could then go to talk to people in order to find information. Busy headteachers and ancillary staff may not welcome a series of children asking them the same questions, but a small group could be managed more easily.

Emphasise the importance of note-taking when the children seek information, and encourage them to organise their notes carefully. When the children have gathered information, ask them to discuss it and compose writing collectively in their groups.

It is important that the guidebooks reach an audience. They might be shown to other classes and members of staff who could offer feedback and suggest useful additions.

Suggestion(s) for extension

A class collection of guidebooks could provide the stimulus for children to produce guides to local places of interest.

Suggestion(s) for support

The co-operative nature of the activity should ensure that everyone is involved, but children who find difficulty with writing should not be restricted to roles as illustrators. Every

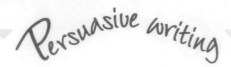
child should be involved in writing in some form even if this is restricted to recording ideas worked out by the group and written with the help of other group members.

Assessment opportunities
Note the children's abilities to use their notes and draft these into well-presented final copy. Look for evidence of careful and attractive presentation. Note their abilities to adopt a persuasive style of writing.

Opportunities for IT
The creation of a guidebook could be linked with a Key Information Technology focus, with children working in small groups to produce their own guidebook using a word processor or desktop publishing package. The children will need to be able to organise and format the writing on the different pages, and select appropriate fonts and styles. They could also include pictures.

A simple format to use is a sheet of A4 paper folded into three vertical columns, so that the six panels provide plenty of opportunities for different information while keeping the task manageable. Alternatively, the class could work together, possibly with an editorial board, and with different groups working on different aspects of the guide.

Display ideas
Display the guidebooks in the school entrance for visitors to look at. A class display of a collection of guidebooks could accompany a display of copies of the children's work.

Other aspects of the English PoS covered
Reading – 1c.

CELEBRITIES

To write to communicate ideas.
Whole class or group, working individually or in pairs.
One hour.

Key background information
This activity is designed to capitalise on children's interest in famous people to promote writing which includes making lists of favourite celebrities and writing justifications for choices.

Preparation
Make sure that there are plenty of pictures of famous people to stimulate children's interests. Cuttings from newspapers and magazines are ideal. Make copies of photocopiable page 153. You will need one copy for each child or pair of children.

Resources needed
Pictures and cuttings from newspapers and magazines, photocopiable page 153, chalkboard, A4 lined paper, scrap paper, pens, pencils.

What to do
Display some of the pictures and photographs and ask the children to brainstorm individually or in pairs to produce lists of as many famous people as they can think of in five minutes. Ask them to read out some of their lists, and write the names of some celebrities on the board to help with spelling. An alternative to this is to ask the children to write the alphabet vertically down the side of a piece of lined paper, with one letter on each line. One child then chooses a number which corresponds to a page in a book, and a second number which corresponds to a line of that page. The first 26 letters of that line are written vertically next to the letters of the alphabet, so that there are 26 pairs of letters.

a	h	*Anthony Hopkins*
b	e	*Ben Elton*
c	l	*Carl Lewis*
d	d	*David Dimbleby*

The children can then be asked to think of a famous person who has the initials which appear on each line. The person or group who think of the most in a set period of time are the winners. Of course it may be difficult or even impossible to think of names for some initials, but the exploration of sound–symbol correspondence which accompanies the children's attempts may be valuable.

Ask the children to think very carefully about their lists and about others people's and decide upon a top ten of their favourites. It may be a good idea to ask them to choose people from different walks of life in order to avoid lists of ten footballers or ten Australian soap opera stars. They can use copies of photocopiable page 153 to make their lists and they should write at least two sentences to justify each choice. The children can write on scrap paper first and then copy their work carefully after checking spellings and punctuation.

The final lists can be read aloud and discussed. In some cases you may be unsure of spellings of names. This should be admitted and possible spellings can be explored with the children. They should be encouraged to find out correct spellings from newspapers and magazines.

Suggestion(s) for extension
The lists could be used as the basis for mathematical work, with children using them to produce a list of the class's favourite celebrities and presenting information in graphs and tables with written commentaries.

Suggestion(s) for support
Provide plenty of pictures to stimulate the enthusiasm of those who do not seem able to think of many celebrities. Some children could be asked to write only one sentence about each celebrity, or they could simply write a few adjectives to describe each person.

Assessment opportunities
Look for examples of careful explanations of choices and appropriate use of adjectives to describe the celebrities. Note phonic awareness in attempts to spell names.

Opportunities for IT
Children should use a desktop publishing package or word processor to present their own number one celebrity, adding a few sentences about each one. If a scanner is available, children could add these pictures to their written work.

Display ideas
Display the lists and explanations, together with photographs of the celebrities. The photographs could be cut in half, the children being presented with one half to complete the pictures of the faces, using pastels.

Other aspects of the English PoS covered
Speaking and listening – 1a; 2a.

Reference to photocopiable sheet
Photocopiable page 153 provides a pro forma for children's lists and justifications of choices.

Celebrities
Name _____ Date _____
▲ Make a list of your ten favourite celebrities. Show your list to your partner and discuss what you like and dislike about each other's choices. Use the space at the side of your list to make notes about your reasons for liking each person. ▲ Now write at least two sentences to go with each name on your list to explain why you like each person. You may use the back of this sheet or another sheet if you need extra space. There are some words at the bottom of the page which you may find useful.

Your top ten	Why do you like that person?
1	
2	
3	
4	
5	
6	
7	
8	
9	
10	

Useful words
famous talented personality beautiful skilful handsome pleasant caring intelligent charismatic

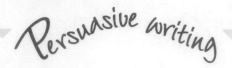

JOB APPLICATIONS

To write in an appropriate style for an extended range of readers.

†† *Whole class or group, working independently.*

⏱ *One hour.*

Key background information

This activity is designed to make formal letter writing purposeful by providing a real audience for it. Children will need to be shown the features of formal letters including: where to write the sender's address; where to write the recipient's address; where to write the date; how to end the letter ('Yours sincerely' if the letter is addressed to a named person and 'Yours faithfully' when it begins 'Dear Sir' or 'Dear Madam').

Preparation

Choose a selection of advertisements for jobs from the local newspaper. If possible, contact the businesses concerned and explain what you are doing and ask if they would mind looking at some of the children's applications and providing feedback. Make copies of the job advertisement on photocopiable page 154, one for each child.

Resources needed

Job advertisements, photocopiable page 154, writing materials, chalkboard.

What to do

Distribute copies of the job advertisement on photocopiable page 154 and ask the children what they would need to include in a letter of application in order to impress the employer. Make a list on the board of their ideas, and then put these together into a letter using the children's comments

throughout. Talk about the ways in which letters are written and explain that this is a formal letter and so it differs from other kinds.

Tell the children that they are going to write letters applying for jobs and provide them with copies of a range of different posts. It may be a good idea to let them choose which job they wish to apply for.

Encourage children to follow the conventions of formal letter writing, and discuss when they should use 'Yours faithfully' and when 'Yours sincerely' is appropriate.

If the work is not to be sent to an employer and you are to respond to it, it is a good idea to write a letter to each child rather than simply marking the work. The letter might include comments on the format of the letter as well as on the applicant's suitability for the job. (The letters could be composed on a word processor with slight amendments made for each child.)

Suggestion(s) for extension

Some children could complete mock application forms, with other children responding to the applications themselves. This might take the form of letters offering interviews or even letters of rejection.

Suggestion(s) for support

Some children may need assistance from an adult to write their letters. It might be pointed out that adults often seek advice on job applications too and that it is quite acceptable to do so.

Assessment opportunities

Note the children's abilities to write in a formal style and to use the devices associated with formal letter writing. Look for examples of appropriate vocabulary choices and neat presentation.

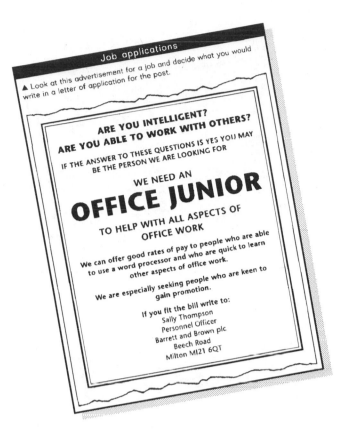

▲ Look at this advertisement for a job and decide what you would write in a letter of application for the post.

Job applications

ARE YOU INTELLIGENT?
ARE YOU ABLE TO WORK WITH OTHERS?
IF THE ANSWER TO THESE QUESTIONS IS YES YOU MAY BE THE PERSON WE ARE LOOKING FOR

WE NEED AN

OFFICE JUNIOR

TO HELP WITH ALL ASPECTS OF OFFICE WORK

We can offer good rates of pay to people who are able to use a word processor and who are quick to learn other aspects of office work.

We are especially seeking people who are keen to gain promotion.

If you fit the bill write to:
Sally Thompson
Personnel Officer
Barrett and Brown plc
Beech Road
Milton MI21 6QT

Opportunities for IT
The children could use a word processor to write, draft and present their letter of application or a curriculum vitae.

Display ideas
Job advertisements could be displayed alongside copies of the children's letters and any responses from businesses or fellow pupils.

Other aspects of the English PoS covered
Reading – 3c.

Reference to photocopiable sheet
Photocopiable page 154 provides a sample job advertisement to be used at the beginning of the activity.

PROBLEM PAGE

To use letter writing for an extended range of readers.
†† *Whole class or groups, working individually or in pairs.*
🕐 *One hour.*

Key background information
This activity is designed to help children to understand that letters can take various forms. Problem pages are a feature of many magazines and newspapers and some children may already have seen them. One of the consistent elements in all problem pages is that correspondents are anonymous.

Preparation
Prepare a display of problem pages appropriate for the age group. It may be necessary to select letters from pages or edit pages, in order to avoid some problems. Draw the children's attention to the display. Make copies of photocopiable page 155, either one for each child or one per pair.

Resources needed
Samples from problem pages of newspapers and magazines, photocopiable page 155, writing materials.

What to do
Introduce the children to the idea of a problem page. Show them the sample problem pages and discuss the answers which are provided. Ask them to think about the sort of problems which might lead to their writing to an agony aunt/ uncle. Then give out copies of photocopiable page 155 and talk about the first example provided on the photocopiable sheet. Ask them how they would have answered the letter. They could discuss this in pairs. Discuss what would be a good and a bad answer.

Ask the children to provide solutions to the second problem on the sheet. They can do this individually or in pairs. Discuss their answers and talk about vocabulary and the need to adopt a sensitive style when dealing with delicate

PAULA'S PROBLEM PAGE

issues. Some children may wish to provide an alternative solution to the first problem, either as well as or instead of the second one.

Suggestion(s) for extension
The class could produce a newspaper with a problem page. Children could invent problems for the page or they could send their own in anonymously.

Suggestion(s) for support
Children who find the activity difficult could write their letters with the aid of a scribe or could work with a partner.

Assessment opportunities
Note the children's abilities to adopt an appropriate style of writing and make appropriate vocabulary choices.

Opportunities for IT
The children could work in groups, using a word processor to write problems for another group to answer, saving the work at each stage. The groups could even swap around so that everyone has a turn at writing and answering letters. The saved versions of the questions and answers could be used to make an 'agony column' in a class newspaper, using a desktop publishing package.

Display ideas
Mount the class newspaper with a problem page on the classroom wall. The problems and their solutions could be displayed, together with published letters.

Other aspects of the English PoS covered
Reading – 1b, c; 2b.

Reference to photocopiable sheet
Photocopiable page 155 provides an example of a problem and a solution as well as a problem for the children to try to solve.

SOUNDS IN SPACE

To write persuasively.

†† *Whole class or group, working individually.*

🕐 *One hour in school plus time at home.*

Key background information
By the time they reach Key Stage 2 most children have begun to take an interest in music. Many will have begun to buy tapes or CDs and some will be learning to play instruments. In this activity they are asked to consider their favourite pieces of music and then to write reasons for their choices.

Preparation
Make copies of photocopiable page 156, one for each child. Prepare a tape of extracts of your own favourite pieces of music if you are going to conclude the activity in this way (see 'What to do').

Resources needed
Photocopiable page 156, chalkboard, writing materials. Cassette player, cassette of extracts of your own favourite pieces of music, cassettes of the children's chosen extracts of music (all optional).

What to do

Discuss with the children the kinds of music that they enjoy. Make notes on the board of some of the artists whom they particularly like and ask them what it is about their songs and tunes which appeals to them. Discuss the way in which some people associate a particular piece of music with a special occasion.

Distribute copies of photocopiable page 156. Explain that you would like the children to imagine that they are going to send a list of their favourite five songs or pieces of music into space in a time capsule. They will be able to write down the titles of their chosen pieces of music on the photocopiable sheet. Encourage them to think of reasons for their choices and ask them to write at least two sentences (on a separate

sheet) to accompany each choice. They might write about a particular part of the song or tune which they like, or they could write about any memories which the music evokes.

It may be a good idea to compile your own list as an example. Extracts from favourite pieces of music could be played too.

Suggestion(s) for extension

Children could work together to compile a class top ten of pieces of music by collating everyone's choices. The results could be represented graphically but with a written commentary to explain findings. Some children may like to copy out extracts of their favourite lyrics from their chosen songs. These could be displayed and others could be invited to identify the songs from which they were taken.

Suggestion(s) for support

Some children may find it difficult to think of sufficient choices of music. If a discussion of the activity is held at the end of

the week, the children can be asked to consider their choices over the weekend before being asked to write about them.

Assessment opportunities

Note the children's abilities to present lists carefully and to write clear explanations for their choices.

Opportunities for IT

The lists of favourite pieces of music and reasons for those choices could be compiled using a word processor. Pictures could be added to give a suitable space/time capsule feel.

The children could also use a multimedia authoring package to create a presentation which could include short extracts of their favourite music. These can be made by using software to record a short section from an audio CD played on the computer's CD-ROM player. These are then saved and added to the presentation, so that by clicking on a suitable word or picture the music is played. Samples of music can take up a lot of disk space, so ten seconds will probably be the maximum that should be recorded. (For music recording copyright contact MCPS, 0181-769-4400.)

Display ideas

Lists could be displayed, together with audio-cassette sleeves, CD sleeves or posters of artists.

Other aspects of the English PoS covered

Speaking and listening – 1d; 2a.

Reference to photocopiable sheet

Photocopiable page 156 provides a sheet for children to write down their selection of music.

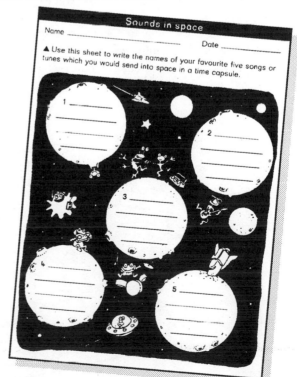

WRITING

THE FILM OF THE BOOK

To write in a style appropriate for justifying choices.

†† *Whole class or group, working in pairs.*

⏰ *30–40 minutes.*

Key background information

Children will almost certainly be familiar with television drama and will have seen cast lists showing which actors played which roles. This activity is designed to be used as a follow-up to a class story. It encourages them to think about the characters in the story and consider which well-known actors and actresses they would ask to play these roles if the book were to be made into a film. They have to write a few lines explaining each of their choices.

Preparation

Bring to school sufficient television magazines for children to be able to refer to them to find the names of actors and actresses from well-known programmes.

Resources needed

Books that the children have read recently, the class story, television magazines, writing materials.

What to do

Show the children cast lists taken from television magazines. Tell the children that they may choose a book which they have enjoyed reading or a book which has been read to them and think about which actors and actresses they would like to see playing the parts of different characters in the story. It may be a good idea to begin by discussing a book which everyone knows.

When the children are ready to begin to cast their book, ask them to justify in a few sentences their choices of actors and actresses. If they wish to cast an actor whose name they do not know, let them use the stage name, but encourage them to find out the name of the actor by looking at television magazines or by watching the credits for the programme at home.

Encourage discussion between children working in pairs and provide periodic breaks for groups to come together and discuss what they are doing.

Suggestion(s) for extension

Children could select a group of actors and write a story which would include those actors playing the leading roles in a film or television version.

Suggestion(s) for support

The main problem children may encounter is a lack of knowledge of the names of actors. Provide photographs and names of well-known actors as a stimulus.

Assessment opportunities

Note the children's abilities to write persuasively when justifying their casting.

Opportunities for IT

The children could use a drawing or art package to design a poster showing the two main actors who are to play the roles in the 'film of the book'. Scanned pictures of the actors could also be included.

Display ideas

Display the cast lists, and put up a sign which invites children to read these and write comments on separate pieces of paper to send to the authors.

Other aspects of the English PoS covered

Reading – 2b.

WRITING

CLASSIFIED ADS

To write concisely and in a style appropriate for a classified ad.

†† *Whole class in pairs.*

🕐 *One hour.*

Key background information

In this activity children will need to be shown how to condense writing so that only minimal information is provided. They will become familiar with the characteristics of writing, such as abbreviations and the use of key words. They will need to see examples of classified ads from newspapers.

Preparation

Make a collection of classified ads from a local newspaper. Make copies of photocopiable page 157; you will need one sheet for each pair.

Resources needed

Examples of classified ads from local and national papers, examples of more detailed advertisements from newspapers and magazines, examples of postcard advertisements of the type placed in shop windows, photocopiable page 157, writing materials.

What to do

Show the children examples of classified ads and explain that people limit the number of words which they use because they have to pay for each word. Show them an example of a longer advertisement, perhaps for a car, taken from a newspaper or a magazine. Explain that the advertiser has paid for space and not for each word, so more information can be provided. Ask the children how they could condense the text for a classified ad of, say, ten words. Provide more examples.

Use the copies of photocopiable page 157 and the examples from the newspapers to show the children different ways in which people advertise what they sell. Explain that, working in pairs, they are going to produce their own advertisements based on those on the photocopiable sheet. Choose products and items which interest the children.

Tell the children that they have a limited budget of, say, £1.50 and that each word will cost 10p. They must include their surname and telephone number, so they have only 13 words available to persuade people to buy their goods.

Discuss the abbreviations which may be used to save words. In car ads, for example, the following tend to appear:

> FSH – full service history
> MOT or MOTC – Ministry of Transport certificate
> VGC – very good condition
> T & T – taxed and tested
> ABS – anti-lock braking system

Suggestion(s) for extension

A class newspaper could be produced, with advertisements placed by children for things which they actually wish to sell or exchange. They could discuss the kinds of words which are left out in classified ads such as conjunctions and articles. They might be asked to reverse the activity, taking classified ads as a basis for producing more detailed advertisements like those which appear in magazines.

Suggestion(s) for support

Children who find the activity difficult could dictate their ideas to a partner. It may help them to work independently if a word bank is provided.

Assessment opportunities

Look for evidence of children being able to write in an appropriate form and note their ability to present their work effectively.

Opportunities for IT

The children could write and edit their classified ad with a word processor, using the word count to check the number of words. Once everyone has written their ad, they can be combined into a newspaper page. This is best undertaken using a desktop publishing package with a single page divided into two or three columns. Each child can then import their ad on to the page. The children could be given the brief to fit all of the ads on to a single page so that they would need to alter the size or style of the font to fit everything in.

Classified ads

▲ Turn these advertisements into classified ads using no more than 15 words including the seller's surname and telephone number.

FOR SALE

1988 Ford Escort with four doors. The car has a stereo radio and a sunroof. It has been well looked after from new and has only had two owners. The engine runs beautifully and the bodywork shows no signs of rust. The car's MOT certificate runs out in October and it is taxed until November. The car also has electric front windows and a tow bar. Reasonable offers around £2000 considered. Contact Louise Chadwick, 01509 466530

FOR SALE

Child's mountain bike. Ideal for 9- to 11-year-old. The cycle is an unwanted Christmas present and has hardly been used. It is in excellent condition. The bike has 10 gears and a speedometer. It also has lights, and a frame bag is included. £65 or near offer or will consider larger bicycle in exchange. Contact Mr S. Douglas, 01896 873007

Display ideas

A class display might incorporate actual advertisements and the children's own efforts. The display could be mounted on a background of newspaper advertisements. A class newspaper could be produced or an advertising journal on the lines of *Exchange and Mart*. Children could add their own illustrations of products.

Other aspects of the English PoS covered

Reading – 1c; 2c.

Reference to photocopiable sheet

Photocopiable page 157 provides two advertisements of the kind one might find in a newsagent's window for children to turn into brief classified ads.

LETTERS TO THE EDITOR

To write persuasively.

†† *Whole class or group, working individually.*

🕐 *At least one hour.*

Previous skills/knowledge needed

This exercise should be undertaken as a form of summative assessment after other activities in this chapter have been completed.

Key background information

Most local and national newspapers feature a 'letters to the editor' page. In this exercise children study these and then reflect on the issues about which they would like to write letters.

Preparation

Find examples of letters pages from newspapers, magazines and comics.

Resources needed

Examples of letters pages, writing materials.

What to do

Show the children a collection of letters pages from a variety of different newspapers and magazines. It may be a good idea to select a few particularly interesting letters to discuss with the whole class. Talk to the children about the kind of language the writers use and the ways in which they try to persuade readers to their point of view. Discuss other types of persuasive writing which the children have attempted and compare them with the letters.

Ask the children to think about an issue which concerns them. It may be a local issue such as a traffic problem, or a school issue such as the wearing of uniform. Alternatively, children might choose to write about a national or international issue such as pollution, crime or famine.

Explain that you want the children to work independently and ask them to keep their letters secret until they can be shared with the whole class.

Suggestion(s) for extension

Children could be asked to write their letter for a particular publication. Discuss with them the differences between letters to some of the broadsheets and some of the local papers and national tabloids.

Suggestion(s) for support

Children who find the activity difficult may be given help by an adult, but this should be noted when recording assessments.

Assessment opportunities

Note how successfully children adopt a persuasive style and their abilities to make appropriate vocabulary choices. Look for evidence of drafting and revising and note children's abilities to write in complete sentences.

Display ideas

The letters might form part of a class newspaper or could be displayed under the heading 'Letters to the Editor', with examples from newspapers placed around the children's work.

Other aspects of the English PoS covered

Speaking and listening – 1a; 2a.
Reading – 1a, b, c; 2b, c.

Photocopiables

The pages in this section can be photocopied for use in the classroom or school which has purchased this book, and do not need to be declared in any return in respect of any photocopying licence.

They comprise a varied selection of both pupil and teacher resources, including pupil worksheets, resource material and record sheets to be completed by the teacher or children. Most of the photocopiable pages are related to individual activities in the book; the name of the activity is indicated at the top of the sheet, together with a page reference indicating where the lesson plan for that activity can be found.

Individual pages are discussed in detail within each lesson plan, accompanied by ideas for adaptation where appropriate – of course, each sheet can be adapted to suit your own needs and those of your class. Sheets can also be coloured, laminated, mounted on to card, enlarged and so on where appropriate.

Pupil worksheets and record sheets have spaces provided for children's names and for noting the date on which each sheet was used. This means that, if so required, they can be included easily within any pupil assessment portfolio.

Incident in the playground, see page 16

Incident in the playground

WRITING

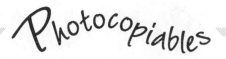
Writing from notes

Thursday, 25th January

8.00am	Got up
8.15am	Had breakfast
8.45am	Went to school
9.00am	Headteacher said school closed – no heating
9.30am	Arrived home
9.45am	Went sledging
10.45am	Arrived at hospital
11.30am	X-rays taken
1.00pm	Arm put in plaster
2.00pm	Arrived home
2.15pm	Ate lunch with one hand
3.30pm	Watched other children sledging

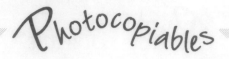

Writing a report, see page 18

Writing a report

Name _____ Date _____

▲ Look at the three headlines. Use the spaces under the headlines to make notes on what you might write for each headline.
▲ Now write a report to go with one of the headlines. Use no more than 200 words. Make sure that your readers want to read on after they have read the first paragraph.

UNITED SAVED BY JONES

STAR QUITS TOP SOAP OPERA

GOVERNMENT ANNOUNCES NEW LAWS ON SCHOOL UNIFORM

Sayings, morals and proverbs, see page 20

Sayings and proverbs

▲ Can you make up a story based upon one of the sayings on this page?

A stitch in time
saves nine.

Two wrongs don't
make a right.

There's no smoke
without fire.

Look before you leap.

It's no use crying
over spilt milk.

Many hands make
light work.

Every cloud has a
silver lining.

Too many cooks
spoil the broth.

It's like looking for a
needle in a haystack.

Actions speak louder
than words.

Don't try to run before
you can walk.

WRITING

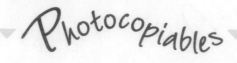

Smarties, see page 22

Smarties

Name _____   Date _____

▲ You will be given a Smartie. It is very important to follow the instructions given below carefully.

---

1 Look at the Smartie, but do not touch it. Make notes on its appearance. Look at the shape and colour. Does it remind you of anything else?

---

2 Now pick the Smartie up and feel it (don't put it in your mouth!). What does it feel like? Jot your ideas down.

---

3 Now comes the most difficult part. You need to put the Smartie in your mouth and suck it and write down notes to describe what that is like. When you can no longer suck the sweet, crunch it and describe what happens. How does the taste change? How does the Smartie feel in your mouth? Make notes.

---

4 When you have finished making your notes, look through them carefully. Is there anything you would like to add or change or get rid of? Now is your chance.

WRITING

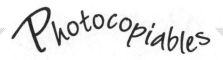
What happened next?

Cinderella sat gazing out of the window watching the droplets of rain slide down the pane like tears on the cheek of an unhappy child. She felt sad. Life would never be quite the same without her sisters.

The funeral had been a simple one with only a handful of mourners. The sisters had had few friends. This was not surprising, since they had spent most of their lives ordering people around and being unpleasant.

Now that Cinderella was twenty-five, she was able to look back on her life with her sisters. Everyone had called them ugly and it was true that they had not been very attractive. They had treated Cinderella badly and had made her do all the housework, but so had the prince whom she had married. In fact, he had sacked all of the servants as soon as they had returned from their honeymoon.

From dawn until dusk all she ever seemed to do was clean and tidy the palace, look after their two children, and wash Prince Charming's smelly socks. He was dreadfully untidy and he never did a thing to help her. He spent every day with his friends hunting, shooting or fishing. Well, she had had enough. He hardly spent any time with the children and he could not change a nappy to save his life.

Prince Charming was anything but charming. 'Prince Useless would have been a better name for him,' thought Cinderella. He never thought about anyone but himself and he was no more fun to live with than her sisters had been. At least they had grown kinder as they grew older. They used to bring presents for the children, Henry and Elizabeth, and they apologised several times for treating their younger sister so unkindly in the past.

That night, Cinderella planned to have a serious talk with her husband. She had decided to take a job and she had no intention of coming home each night to do the housework. He would either have to employ a housekeeper and a nanny or he would have to stay at home and cook, clean and look after the children himself.

Mini sagas

▲ Look at the mini sagas on this page. Each story is written in 50 words.

Jack and the Beanstalk

There was no money. Jack's mother told him to sell the cow. He swapped the cow for beans. Furious, his mother threw them out, but they grew into a beanstalk which Jack climbed. The giant at the top had gold which Jack stole before descending and chopping down the beanstalk.

Goldilocks and the Three Bears

Three bears, Mummy, Daddy and Baby, awoke. Breakfast was too hot, so they took a walk. Goldilocks, little girl, sneaked into their house, ate their porridge, sat on their chairs and broke Baby Bear's. She slept on the small bear's bed, but ran away in terror when the family returned.

Cinderella

Cinderella did housework. Her ugly sisters went to a dance. Her fairy godmother appeared, gave her coach, clothes and horses. Cinders went to the dance and met the prince. At midnight Cinders lost everything, but the prince found one shoe. He found Cinderella. The shoe fitted, so he married her.

▲ Try to write your own version of a well-known story in exactly 50 words. You could choose one of the stories below or you could make up one of your own.

Little Red Riding Hood   The Town Mouse and the Country Mouse   Aladdin
The Three Little Pigs   Hansel and Gretel

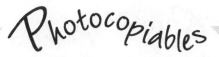

A million pounds, see page 39

If I had a million pounds

Name _____   Date _____

▲ Use the sections on this sheet to help you to make notes.

What I would buy for myself:

What I would buy for my family:

What I would buy for my friends:

What I would do to help other people:

Would having so much money make me happy?

WRITING

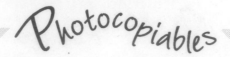
Limericks

Name _____   Date _____

▲ Look at the incomplete limericks and try to finish them off.

There was an old lady from Cork,
Who wanted to fly like a hawk.
She made herself wings
From blankets and things,
_____

There once was a young boy named Dave,
Who didn't know how to behave.
He acted the fool
Each day at his school,
_____

There was a young man from Stoke,

Who _____

_____

_____

_____

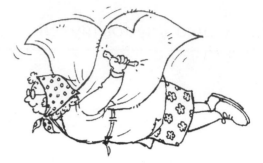

There once was a girl name of Jill,

Who _____

She went out to the shop

And _____

_____

Haiku

▲ Here are some examples of haiku. Look at the way in which each has five syllables on the first line, seven on the second, and five on the third.

A wooden toy sold
Yet more trees fall to the ground.
The Earth's lifeblood sapped.

Bath deep, hot, steaming.
Step in, warmth on skin,
Relaxing, soothing.

The river runs deep,
After it started so steep,
Then dies at the sea.

Eyes still and longing,
But thoughts spiralling and loud.
Will sleep ever come?

Beautiful feline.
Stalk your unsuspecting prey.
So quiet, so deadly.

Days grow short, nights long.
Leaves in autumn hues once more,
Dancing in the wind.

Watching the moon rise,
Seeing the western sun fade,
My worries lie down.

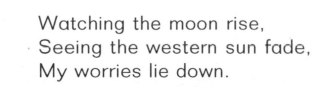

Telegram notes

▲ Look at the examples of telegrams below and try to rewrite them in sentences, adding more details.

TO: BLACKBURN ROVERS

WANT TO BUY SHEARER FOR UNITED STOP

WILL PAY £10 MILLION STOP

MUST SIGN BEFORE THURSDAY STOP

PLEASE REPLY IMMEDIATELY STOP

FROM: MANAGER, SCUNTHORPE UNITED

TO: PC A DIBBLE

LION ESCAPED STOP

HEADING YOUR WAY STOP

STAY INDOORS STOP

DO NOT SHOOT STOP

ZOO WILL RECAPTURE STOP

FROM: HEAD ZOO-KEEPER

TO: MRS S BROWNE

NEED HELP STOP

NO MONEY STOP

NO FOOD STOP

PLEASE SEND MONEY IMMEDIATELY STOP

WILL PAY BACK LATER STOP

FROM: DAVID

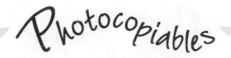

Did you know that?

Name _____   Date _____

▲ Look at the facts below and then try to find some more to fill in the empty boxes.

> The first people to fly were the Marquis d'Arlandes and Pilâtre de Rozier in 1783. Their hot-air balloon had a straw-burning fire underneath it!

> An Italian called Marconi transmitted the first radio signal across the Atlantic in 1901.

> The diesel engine was invented by Rudolf Diesel, a German who was nearly killed when his first engine exploded. Diesel disappeared mysteriously from the Harwich steam ferry on his way to London.

> Joseph Haydn's *Miracle Symphony* is so called because, at the end of its first performance, the audience rushed forward to congratulate him and a large chandelier fell from the ceiling. If they had not moved many would have been killed.

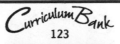

Neighbours, see page 54

Neighbours

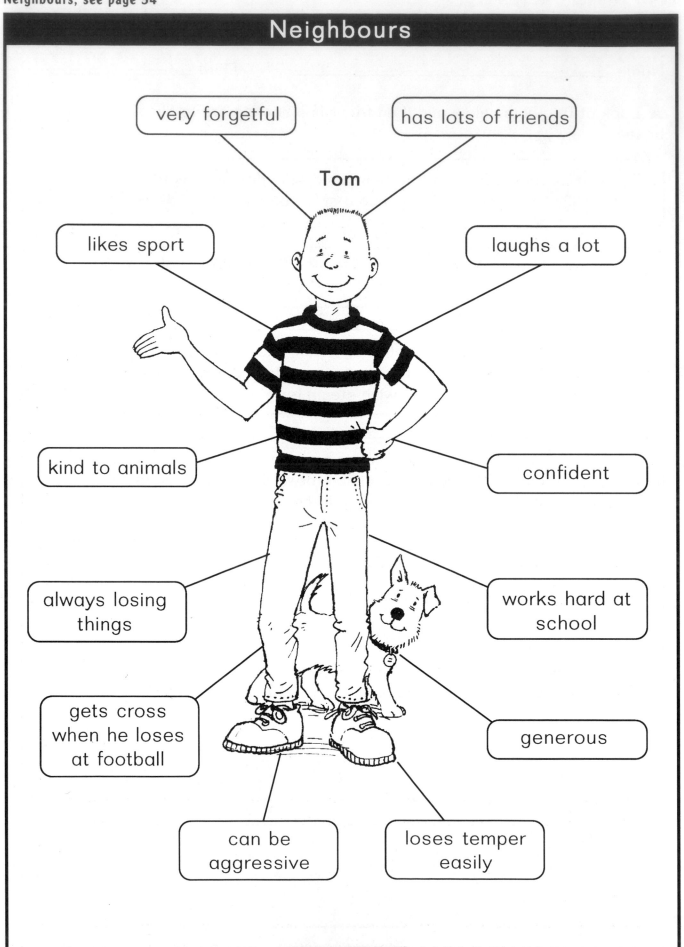

Tom

very forgetful

has lots of friends

likes sport

laughs a lot

kind to animals

confident

always losing things

works hard at school

gets cross when he loses at football

generous

can be aggressive

loses temper easily

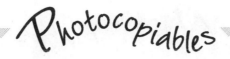

Preparing a talk to the class, see page 56

Preparing a talk to the class

Name _____ Date _____

▲ Look at the list of topics below. You may choose one of them for your talk or you may decide to talk about another topic of your choice.

Migration	Day and night	Keeping a pet
Our town/village	How something works	Growing things
An author	A king or queen	A religious festival
A holiday	Another country	A type of animal
Transport	Space flights	A sport

▲ The sections below are intended to help you to organise your talk.

Introduction – How will you get the audience interested?

Things you will show to the audience

Main pieces of information

Conclusion – How you will finish off your talk.

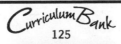
WRITING

Flow charts

Name _____   Date _____

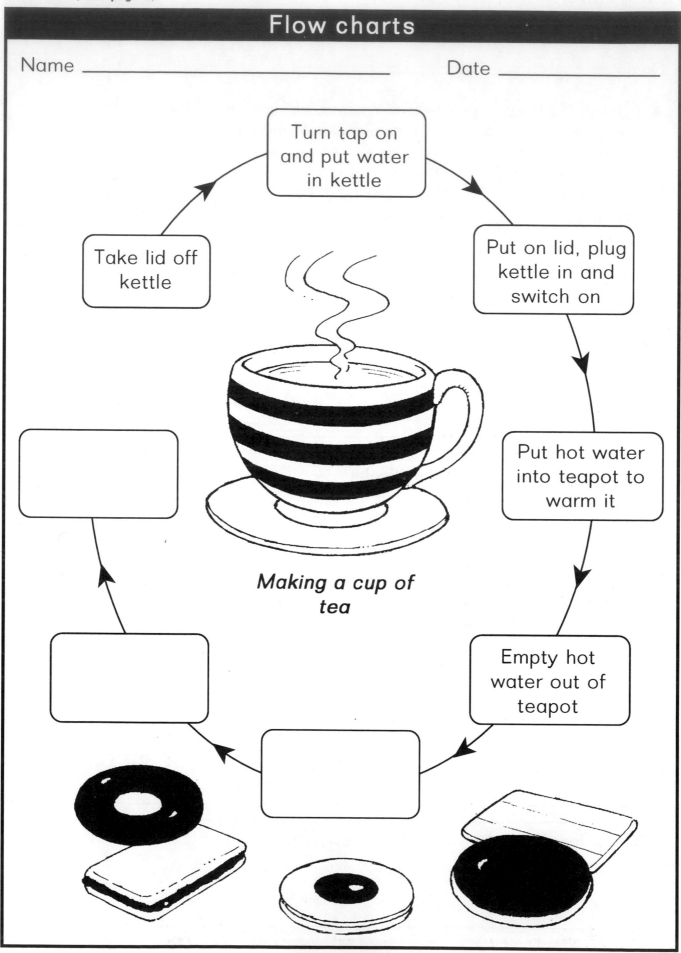

Turn tap on and put water in kettle

Take lid off kettle

Put on lid, plug kettle in and switch on

Put hot water into teapot to warm it

Empty hot water out of teapot

Making a cup of tea

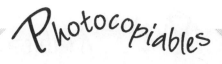

Photocopiables

Questionnaire (1)

Name _____   Date _____

▲ This questionnaire is intended to find information about children's leisure interests. All replies will be treated as confidential. Names and addresses are required for administrative purposes.

Please answer the following questions in black ink in block capital letters.

Full name _____

Gender (male/female) _____

Address _____

Street _____

Town _____ Postcode _____

Please answer the following questions by ticking the most suitable answers.

1 Which of these sports do you play in most weeks? (Please tick those which apply.)

☐ Athletics   ☐ Hockey   ☐ Tennis

☐ Cricket   ☐ Judo   ☐ Other (please state)

☐ Football   ☐ Netball   _____

☐ Golf   ☐ Rounders   _____

☐ Gymnastics   ☐ Rugby   ☐ None

2 How many hours do you spend watching television on an average school day? (Please tick one.)

☐ Less than 1 hour   ☐ Between 3 and 4 hours

☐ Between 1 and 2 hours   ☐ More than 4 hours

☐ Between 2 and 3 hours

Curriculum Bank

127

WRITING

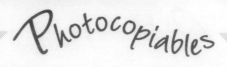
Questionnaire (2)

3 How many hours do you spend listening to the radio or listening to music on a cassette player or CD player on an average school day? (Please tick one.)

☐ Less than 1 hour   ☐ Between 3 and 4 hours

☐ Between 1 and 2 hours   ☐ More than 4 hours

☐ Between 2 and 3 hours

4 How many hours do you spend reading at home on an average school day? (Please tick one.)

☐ Less than 1 hour   ☐ Between 3 and 4 hours

☐ Between 1 and 2 hours   ☐ More than 4 hours

☐ Between 2 and 3 hours

5 Do you have any of the following leisure interests? (Please tick those which apply.)

☐ Ballet/dance   ☐ Ice-skating

☐ Board games
(eg. chess, draughts, Scrabble)   ☐ Making models
(eg. LEGO, Meccano, Airfix)

☐ Card games   ☐ Playing a musical instrument

☐ Computer games   ☐ Snooker/pool

☐ Cycling   ☐ Swimming

☐ Drawing/painting   ☐ Horse riding

☐ Other (please state) _____

Thank you for taking the time and trouble to answer the questions.

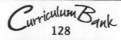

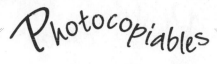

Four-letter words

Name _____   Date _____

▲ Can you add to the list?

been	best	book	came	come	does
each	ever	find	from	game	gave
give	goes	good	have	head	help
here	high	home	just	keep	kept
knew	know	lady	last	left	live
lost	many	more	much	must	name
nice	once	only	open	over	play
real	said	same	show	soon	stay
take	talk	than	that	then	they
this	time	told	used	very	walk
week	went	were	what	when	will
wish	work	year	your		

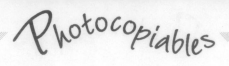

Combining sentences

Name _____   Date _____

▲ Can you join the sentences in each group so that there are fewer sentences? You may add words or take words away.

Group 1
Dominic has a bicycle.
Sophie has a bicycle.
Raj has a football.
Nicola has a tennis ball.

Group 2
The wind blew.
The rain fell heavily.
Asif was fast asleep.
Lee could not sleep.

Group 3
The dog awoke.
It scratched itself.
It shook itself.
The dog went to look for
something to eat.
There was nothing in its bowl.
The dog began to bark.

Group 4
Harold and his men looked down
on William's men from the top of
the hill.
William had a cunning plan.
William's men fired arrows high
into the air.
One of the arrows hit Harold.
Harold was killed.
William's army had won the battle.

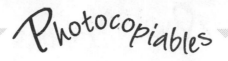
Unfinished sentences

Name _____   Date _____

▲ Can you complete the sentences? Try to make the sentences as interesting as possible.

1 The car's tyres screeched as _____

_____

2 A gust of wind picked up the baseball cap and _____

_____

3 I don't care if I never _____

_____

4 Ben felt himself falling as he _____

_____

5 Holly opened the sack and pulled out a _____

_____

6 Every eye in the room looked at him as he _____

_____

7 My favourite game is_____

_____

8 The noise was deafening, but Rebecca knew she had to ____

_____

9 Although he was often silly, Nicholas was _____

_____

10 I made sure no one was looking and then I _____

_____

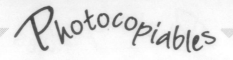

What was the question?

Name _____   Date _____

▲ So *that's* the answer! Now, what was the question? Can you think of exciting and imaginative questions for each of these five answers?

> **1** It's Lauren's birthday tomorrow.

> **2** It was hiding in the wood.

> **3** Everybody says the place is haunted.

> **4** The roller-coaster, please!

> **5** No, I had never seen him before.

> **6** There's a strange creature floating in it.

> **7** It just seemed to disappear.

> **8** I was absolutely terrified.

WRITING

Commas, see page 72

The comma that saved a human life

The Czar of Russia was a powerful ruler who had many enemies. Whenever he caught one of them, he ordered the unfortunate person to be sent to Siberia, a distant, dark and cold land. Few prisoners who went there ever returned.

One dark winter's night, one such prisoner was waiting, shivering, on the station in Moscow, the capital city of the Czar's Empire. His friends had made a last-minute, desperate appeal to the Czar to set the prisoner free. The prisoner and his guards were waiting anxiously to hear whether or not the appeal had been successful.

The seconds ticked away. Any minute now, the train for Siberia would depart, taking the prisoner away from the home he loved. Meanwhile, in the Czar's palace, a life-or-death decision was being made. The Czar ordered his secretary to write the following words: **Pardon impossible, to be sent to Siberia.** It seemed the prisoner's fate was sealed. However, the secretary made a slight slip of the pen. This is what he actually wrote: **Pardon, impossible to be sent to Siberia.**

The message was delivered to the guards at the station. They read it, shrugged, and released their prisoner. And that is the story of how a comma saved a human life!

WRITING

Commas, see page 72

Missing commas

Name _____ Date _____

▲ Can you put the missing commas in these sentences?

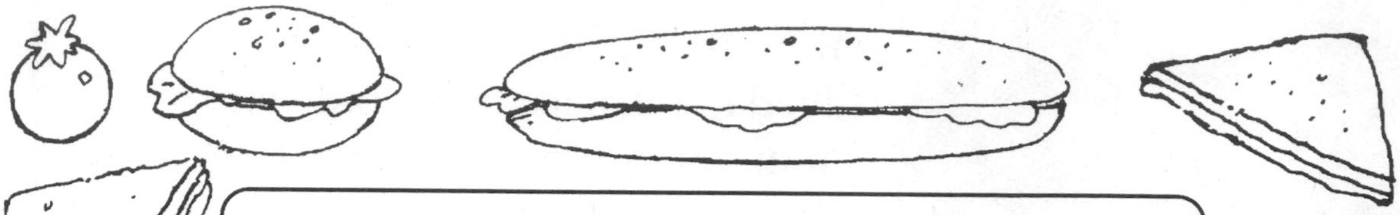

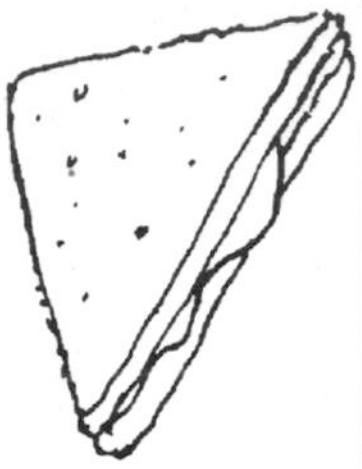

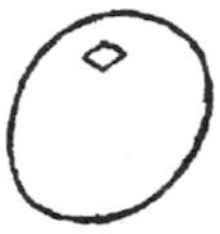

1 The shop sells beef ham cheese tomato and egg sandwiches.
(Commas for lists)

2 Can you pay the bill Bill?
(Comma separates the name of the person being spoken to from the rest of the sentence)

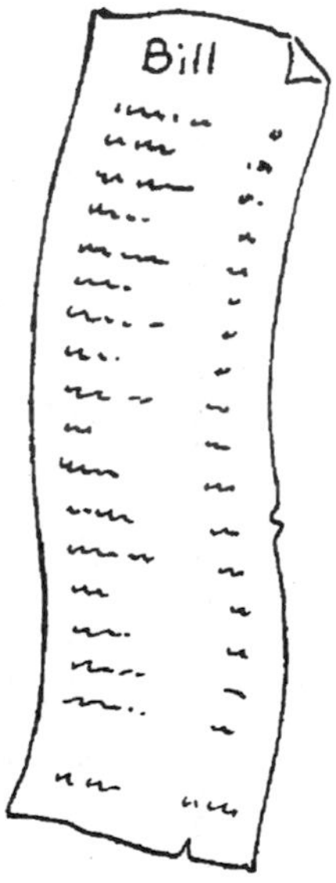

3 Suddenly there was a loud noise.
(Adverbial at the start of the sentence)

4 Their pets however had to stay at home.
(Adverbial in the middle of the sentence)

5 She has not been badly hurt luckily.
(Adverbial at the end of the sentence)

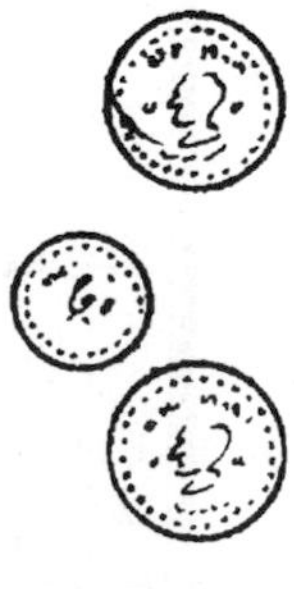

... and what about this?!

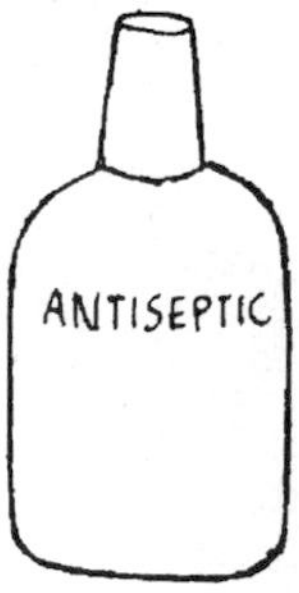

6 Can you dry Jonathan?

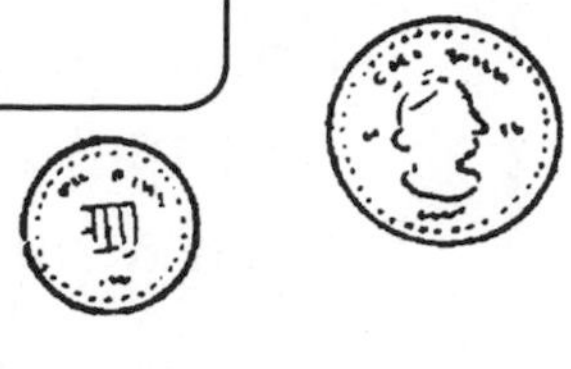

ANTISEPTIC

Bill

BANG

Paragraphs, see page 76

Stepping-stones story

1 It was Hallowe'en. The night was cold and stormy. The wind howled across the moor, shaking the leafless trees so that they seemed to dance in the moonlight. The sound of thunder boomed suddenly through the darkness.

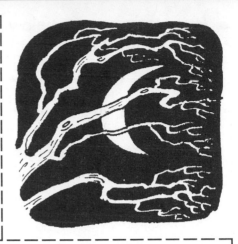

2 An old man, trudging wearily through the rain-soaked heather, heard the noise. Slowly and painfully, he raised his head just in time to see a fork of lightning flash against the walls of a ruined tower. Through the darkness and the rain, he could dimly see the light of a flickering candle high in the window.

3 Something drew the old man onwards towards that flickering light. Closer and closer he came. Louder and louder blew the storm. Now he was at the door to the ruined tower. He wanted to turn and run but he could not move. Slowly the tower door creaked open. A threatening figure stood before him. The figure spoke. 'Five pints of blue-top, Albert! Why's the milk so late? You'd better have a good excuse this time!'

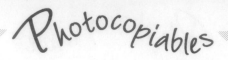

Pronouns, see page 77

Pronouns

▲ Read the passage below. How could it be improved? Write your new version on a separate sheet of paper.

Jenny was always smiling. Jenny was a very happy little girl and Jenny was never sad. Jenny had a brother called Daniel. Daniel was younger than Jenny. Daniel smiled a lot, but sometimes Daniel cried when he wanted some milk or when his nappy needed to be changed.

Jenny's mummy and daddy were very happy too. Her mummy was a bus driver. Jenny's mummy drove big double-decker buses. Jenny's daddy worked in a factory. Jenny's daddy helped to make cars. Jenny wanted to make buses when she grew up.

▲ Can you use pronouns to improve this piece of writing about Robert and Rover? Use a separate sheet of paper.

Robert's dog was called Rover. Robert really liked Rover. Robert used to take Rover into the park and throw sticks for him. Rover refused to fetch the sticks back to Robert so Robert tried throwing balls instead. Rover would not fetch balls either and Robert lost a lot of balls playing with Rover.

Robert tried to teach Rover other tricks. Robert tried to teach Rover to sit up and beg, but Rover would not sit up and beg. Robert tried to teach Rover to fetch the newspaper from the shop, but Rover just lay in front of the fire.

Some people said that Rover was not a very clever dog because he would not run around fetching things and because he would not sit up and beg. Robert thought that Rover was very clever because he would not run around fetching things and because he would not sit up and beg.

WRITING

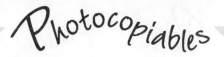

Yorkshire farm labourers

Dialect version

R.M. Hello, Alf. Wheer ta for? Off a bit?
I see thou'rt dolled up.

A.M. Nay, not far, I'm just walkin' out a
bit, that's all. Tha sees I'm out
o'work ageean.

Standard English version

R.M. Hello, Alf. Where are you going?
Is it far? I notice that you're smartly
dressed.

A.M. No, not far, I'm just going for a little
stroll, that's all. I'm out of work
again, you know.

WRITING

Apostrophes for abbreviation, see page 83

Our planet

Name _____   Date _____

▲ Read the writing below and underline the words which have been shortened by using apostrophes. Write the longer version of the words above the shortened versions.

It isn't long since people thought that the Earth was flat

and that if you sailed far enough you'd fall off the edge.

We'd probably still think the Earth was flat if it wasn't

for the explorations made by people like Francis Drake

who sailed around the world. We've even seen pictures of the Earth beamed

to us by satellite and we can see that it's more or less spherical in shape.

Our ancestors wouldn't have believed it possible

that people could fly in spaceships and take

pictures of our planet. They'd've been amazed

that we could fly at all. It's less than a hundred

years since the first powered aeroplane flew, so

we've come a long way in a short time.

It can't be long before people fly to other planets or to distant stars. It's

hard to imagine this, but our ancestors couldn't've imagined people sailing

all the way around the Earth!

Apostrophes for possession, see page 84

Apostrophes for possession (1)

▲ Here are some examples of apostrophes being used to denote possession.

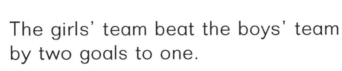

Jim's car was faster than James's.

The girls' team beat the boys' team by two goals to one.

The lady's coat was red.

The ladies' cloakroom was closed.

The children's clothes were wet.

Anne's favourite food was bananas.

The trout's skin was brown.

The men's room was full.

She was Britain's first world champion in the event.

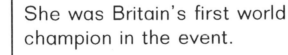

The doctor's car was parked outside Mr Brown's house.

The boys' changing room was locked.

Susan's son's hair was longer than Tony's daughter's.

Mrs Milford's house was full of her husband's clothes.

He painted the car's wheels silver.

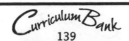

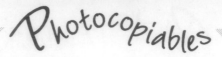
Apostrophes for possession, see page 84

Apostrophes for possession (2)

Name _____ Date _____

▲ Can you put apostrophes in the right places in the sentences below?

Matthews dog was stuck in the mud.

Sarahs mother was waiting for her at the school gates.

The boys shoe was lost.

The boys toilets were locked.

The birds nests were high in the trees.

Mr Dawsons car was brand new.

Carrots, cabbages and potatoes were Nicks favourite vegetables.

The teachers jacket was hanging on a coat hanger.

The teachers classrooms were their pride and joy.

Rovers goal was one of the best Citys goalkeeper had ever seen.

Bills came through Bills letter-box every day.

The soggy tomatos skin was wrinkled.

The potatoes skins were burnt and black.

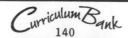
WRITING

Nonsense sentences, see page 87

Nonsense sentences

The silly sausage hit the red banana.
The clever bicycle kissed the funny dishwasher.
The old baby bit the lazy chair.
The dead table caught the wooden man.
The pretty house kicked the empty carrot.

A happy wardrobe carefully laughed at the bent classroom.
An amazing turnip quickly jumped on the hard sum.
A tired tent kindly sang to the intelligent tree.
A rich pea sadly ran to the young window.
A beautiful sock stupidly drank from the handsome hedge.

The stupid, orange dog silently ate the large, pink umbrella.
The intelligent, blue strawberry reluctantly called the tall, frightened flower.
The sad, clever tree happily played the hopeless, beautiful coat.
The kind, sensible train hardly ate the fair, green house.
The slow, fat aeroplane quickly bought the dead, yellow drainpipe.

WRITING

Use of adjectives, see page 88

Use of adjectives (1)

Name _____ Date _____

▲ Can you make the writing below more interesting by adding adjectives to describe people and things? One has been done for you.

young

The boy had a coat on because it was windy. Rain began to fall as he walked down the road to his grandmother's house. He liked going to his grandmother's house. She often gave him chocolate and sweets and she made his lunch. He hoped that she would be cooking chicken and chips when he arrived. He was not allowed to eat chips at home. His mother and father said they would make him fat.

He really liked the front door at his grandmother's house. It had a knocker and a bell and he liked to knock with the knocker and ring the bell at the same time. His parents would be cross if he did that at home, but his grandmother didn't mind.

▲ Now add another paragraph to continue the passage, using the back of this sheet. Include adjectives in your writing to make it interesting for readers.

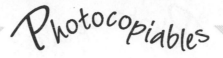

Use of adjectives, see page 88

Use of adjectives (2)

Name _____   Date _____

▲ Can you make the writing below more interesting by adding adjectives to describe people and things?

The ship sailed on the sea. It sailed through the storm. The people on board looked at the sky and at the waves. They were afraid. Some people thought that the ship might sink.

The captain of the ship scratched his head and looked at the sea. 'I don't like the look of it,' he said. 'I can see a light on the horizon, but we have to sail through the waves to get home.'

He listened to the wind and looked at the rain. 'I think we will get home safely, but it's going to be difficult on this sea,' he said.

Just as the captain spoke a wave crashed over the top of the ship and the wind grew stronger. The passengers heard a noise and a man noticed that water was coming into his cabin.

▲ Now add another paragraph to continue the passage, using the back of this sheet. Include adjectives in your writing to make it interesting for readers.

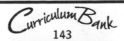
WRITING

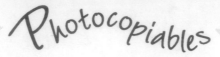
Similes: painting pictures in words

Name _____ Date _____

▲ Poets are especially good at using similes to paint pictures in words. Read these four extracts and listen carefully to what your teacher tells you about them. Can you write imaginative words to make the similes complete?

From *Sleeping Cats* by Moira Andrew

Cats dedicate their lives to dozing,

Stretched out like _____

From *For F.E.H.* by Frances Horovitz

The old man stretched on his bed, weightless as _____

_____

From *Aeroplane* by Celia Warren

Like a _____

a vapour cuts cleanly through the blue;

the only white in a cloudless day

From *Gift from the Stars* by John Rice

Their eyes are distant and blue, like _____

Their silky robes flow like _____

▲ When you have finished, can you say why you chose the words you did? Write a sentence for each of the four extracts.

▲ When your teacher tells you the words that the poets used, can you say which you prefer – your similes or theirs? Write a sentence for each of the four extracts.

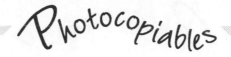

Onomatopoeia, see page 91

Onomatopoeia

Name _____   Date _____

▲ Can you fill in the spaces using onomatopoeic words?

Oliver hurried down the stairs and ran towards the kitchen. He was afraid.

He had heard a loud _____ from the room and he wondered what

had happened.

As he walked into the kitchen he saw his sister drop a plate. It went

_____ on the floor. 'Oh no, that's another one!' said Hannah.

'Every time I wash up I seem to _____ the crockery.

Oliver went to the sink to help, but another plate dropped into the water

with a _____. He felt the bits of broken plate _____ under

his shoes as he walked to the cupboard to fetch a dustpan and brush.

His sister let the water out of the sink and Oliver heard it _____

down the plug hole. The floor was wet and messy. 'Let's have a drink,' said

Hannah. She put orange squash into two glasses and turned on the tap.

The water _____ out of the tap and _____ into the glasses.

'It's almost as wet in here as it is outside,' said Oliver. Outside the wind

_____ and the rain _____ on to the pavement.

'Let's clear up before Mum and Dad find us,' whispered Hannah. 'I think

I heard a door _____ing upstairs.'

Précis, see page 92

Précis

▲ Look at the way that the information which is written in 150 words can be written in 80 words. Can you rewrite it in fewer words without removing any important information?

The Beatles were a very popular group in the 1960s. Millions of people all over the world bought their records and copied their hairstyles. Most of their songs were written by John Lennon and Paul McCartney, but some were written by George Harrison and Ringo Starr.

The group came from Liverpool and some people even tried to talk with Liverpool accents to copy the Beatles. People screamed and fainted at their concerts.

Ringo was the drummer and his real name was Richard Starkey. He was called Ringo because he wore so many rings. The other group members played guitars. John also played the mouth organ and Paul sometimes played the piano.

The Beatles' songs are still heard today. They include 'I Want to Hold Your Hand', 'Yesterday', 'Let it Be' and 'Yellow Submarine'.

Unfortunately, John Lennon was killed in 1980, but the other members of the group still make records.

Liverpool group, The Beatles, were very popular in the 1960s. People copied their accents and hairstyles and screamed and fainted at their concerts.

Guitarists John Lennon and Paul McCartney wrote most of the songs, but guitarist, George Harrison, and drummer, Ringo Starr, whose real name was Richard Starkey, wrote some.

Their songs, which include 'I Want to Hold Your Hand', 'Yesterday', and 'Let it Be' can still be heard. John was killed in 1980, but the others still make records.

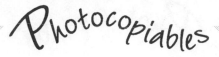
Turning a drama script into prose, see page 93

Turning a drama script into prose

▲ Read the script and then rewrite it in prose.

MRS SMITH	Sam, are you ready for school yet?
SAM *(calling)*	I can't come down, Mum.
MRS SMITH	Whatever is the matter, Sam?
SAM	I'm stuck!
MRS SMITH *(running up the stairs)*	What do you mean you're stuck? What have you done? *(She sees Sam)* Oh no!
SAM	I'm sorry, Mum. I didn't mean to do it.
MRS SMITH	You silly boy! Why did you put your toe in the tap in the first place? It can't have been an accident.
SAM *(crying)*	I didn't mean to, honestly. It just sort of happened.
MRS SMITH	Well, I'm going downstairs to phone the fire brigade. They'll know how to get you out. Don't go away!
SAM *(shouting)*	Oh please don't ring them, Mum. I don't want a lot of fireman to see me in the bath!
MRS SMITH	You should have thought of that before you got your toe stuck in the tap.

(Mrs Smith goes out of the room and picks up the telephone. She presses three times on the same button.)

MRS SMITH	Hello... yes, fire brigade please... yes, I'll hold on. Hello, Fire Brigade? Yes, I'm sorry to bother you, but it's my son... No he hasn't lit a fire, he's got his toe stuck in the bath tap... Yes, that's what I said to him. You'll come round and see what you can do... Oh thank you... 23 Spring Road... Right, I'll see you in a few minutes. Oh, you won't be coming yourself, your mates will... All right. Thank you very much. Goodbye.

▲ Can you finish the story? Write in script form or in prose.

WRITING

Fortunately/unfortunately

▲ Can you write a fortunately/unfortunately story with a partner? The one below may give you some ideas.

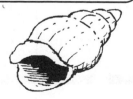

Fortunately, I am going on holiday next week.

Unfortunately, I do not have a swimming costume and we are going to the seaside.

Fortunately, I have saved up enough money to buy one.

Unfortunately, the shop has sold out of swimming costumes.

Fortunately, I think that there is a shop which sells them at the seaside.

Unfortunately, the costumes the shop sells are all made for adults.

Fortunately, I am quite big for my age and an adult size might fit me.

Unfortunately, when my big brother bought an adult-sized costume my dad borrowed it.

Fortunately, I am a girl and I don't think he would look very good in a bikini!

WRITING

Bank robbery, see page 96

Newspaper report

▲ Read the report carefully. Imagine that you were one of the people mentioned in the report and write in detail about what you saw and did.

BANK ROBBERS FOILED!

By Peter Lant

Bentley's Bank in Middleford was yesterday the scene of an act of incredible bravery on the part of two young children.

Mark and Joanne Ward were accompanying their father as he withdrew money from his account, when a gang of four armed robbers burst into the bank and ordered customers to lie on the floor.

Cashiers were told to fill the robbers' bags with money, while the villains waved guns menacingly at the frightened customers. However, Joanne, aged eleven, spotted that the pistols the men were carrying were the same as the ones her cousins played with. In other words, they were toy guns! She decided to call the men's bluff and stood up and shouted to the cashiers not to fill the bags because the guns were only toys.

Mrs Elsie Sandford, who was one of the people lying on the floor, told our reporter: 'Everyone told the little girl to be quiet and shut up and one of the robbers threatened to shoot her, but she just walked over to him and put her finger in the barrel. Her brother did the same. It was amazing – the robbers didn't know what to do!'

Detective Sergeant Steven Dix told us: 'Once the robbers realised that no one was taking them seriously they fled, leaving their toy guns behind them. These children were very brave.'

Bank manager Raymond Kirby said that the children's actions had saved the bank thousands of pounds and added, 'I am sure that Head Office will be issuing a reward.'

The robbers drove away at speed in a blue Ford van, but were later apprehended by police when they ran out of petrol. According to Detective Sergeant Dix, 'They were not the cleverest thieves we have ever known!'

Joanne told us that she did not feel brave at all. 'It was obvious that the guns were fakes,' she said. Mark, aged nine, added, 'I could hardly stop laughing when I saw them. I thought they were playing a practical joke.'

Mr Ward, however, had mixed feelings about his children's actions. 'I suppose they were brave, but what if the guns had been real. I have told them that sometimes it is better to be cowardly and stay safe.'

Last night four men were helping the police with their inquiries.

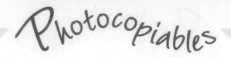

Bank robbery, see page 96

Language study assessment sheet

Name: Age: Date:	
Languages spoken:	
Comment on the child's ability to:	
▲ plan, draft, revise and proofread	
▲ use full stops appropriately	
▲ use commas appropriately	
▲ use question marks appropriately	
▲ punctuate direct speech	
▲ use apostrophes to mark possession	
▲ use apostrophes to spell shortened forms of words	
▲ use knowledge of word structure to help with spelling	
▲ use dictionaries etc. to help with spelling	
▲ make use of adverbs, adjectives and pronouns to enhance writing	
▲ make interesting and appropriate vocabulary choices	

WRITING

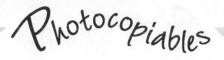

Fact or opinion?, see page 98

Fact or opinion?

Name _____ Date _____

	Fact	Opinion
1 The Battle of Hastings was fought in 1066.	☐	☐
2 I think that's a brilliant idea!	☐	☐
3 Acorns grow on oak trees.	☐	☐
4 Chocolate is the best flavour for ice-cream.	☐	☐
5 York is an interesting city to visit.	☐	☐
6 York is a popular city for visitors.	☐	☐
7 You should always put on a coat when you go out.	☐	☐
8 Matilda is a beautiful name.	☐	☐
9 The Pacific is the biggest ocean in the world.	☐	☐
10 Dogs make better pets than cats.	☐	☐

Fact or opinion?, see page 98

Anytown Pleasure Park

ADVERTISEMENT FEATURE

COME TO ANYTOWN PLEASURE PARK FOR THE HOLIDAY OF A LIFETIME!

Anytown Pleasure Park lies five miles outside the seaside resort of Anytown,  a popular holiday centre in the north of England, where the sun always shines and the rain never falls and the beaches are always full of happy, smiling children!

Anytown Pleasure Park promises you the holiday of a lifetime where all your dreams are guaranteed to come true! Our 'Big Dipper'

is the largest in the country – you'll tingle with fear just at the sight of it! Or why not try a relaxing row on the lake? Birds from many distant lands come to nest on its shores. The sound of their singing is like music to the ears!

So, whatever your pleasure, we promise to satisfy your every wish. Whether you're eight or eighty-eight, Anytown Pleasure Park promises you the holiday of a lifetime.

WRITING

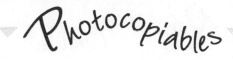
Celebrities

Name _____   Date _____

▲ Make a list of your ten favourite celebrities. Show your list to your partner and discuss what you like and dislike about each other's choices. Use the space at the side of your list to make notes about your reasons for liking each person.

▲ Now write at least two sentences to go with each name on your list to explain why you like each person. You may use the back of this sheet or another sheet if you need extra space. There are some words at the bottom of the page which you may find useful.

Your top ten	Why do you like that person?
1	
2	
3	
4	
5	
6	
7	
8	
9	
10	

Useful words

famous	personality	skilful	pleasant	intelligent
talented	beautiful	handsome	caring	charismatic

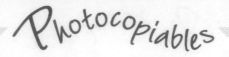

Job applications

▲ Look at this advertisement for a job and decide what you would write in a letter of application for the post.

ARE YOU INTELLIGENT?
ARE YOU ABLE TO WORK WITH OTHERS?

IF THE ANSWER TO THESE QUESTIONS IS YES YOU MAY BE THE PERSON WE ARE LOOKING FOR

WE NEED AN

OFFICE JUNIOR

TO HELP WITH ALL ASPECTS OF OFFICE WORK

We can offer good rates of pay to people who are able to use a word processor and who are quick to learn other aspects of office work.

We are especially seeking people who are keen to gain promotion.

If you fit the bill write to:
Sally Thompson
Personnel Officer
Barrett and Brown plc
Beech Road
Milton MI21 6QT

WRITING

Problem page, see page 105

Paula's problem page

▲ Look at the problems below. The first one has an answer. Do you agree with it? The second problem does not have a solution. Can you write one?

Dear Paula

I am writing to you because I am very worried. My friends don't seem to like me any more. I used to have lots of friends and we always played together, but ever since my family moved house they have not called for me.

Our new house is only a mile from the old one, but my friends don't seem to want to walk that far to see me. There are lots of children from my school in our new street, but I haven't made friends with any of them.

I really wish that I had someone to play with and I am bored. What can I do?

Yours sincerely

Luke

Dear Luke

I am sorry that you are unhappy, but I think the solution to your problem is easy. You must make the effort to make friends with the children who live near to your new house.

It can be very difficult to make friends if you don't try hard. What you should do is go out and ask if you can join in with their games. They might be a bit reluctant at first, but if you take some sweets with you I'm sure that they will make you welcome!

It's no good grumbling that your old friends don't want to come and see you. Have you thought of going to see them? If your friends are worth having it is worth making an effort to see them.

Why not ask your parents if you can invite people to your house for a party or just to come to play? You could invite your old friends and your new friends.

Don't sit at home and grumble about your lack of friends. Go out and do something about it!
Paula

Dear Paula

I have a terrible problem. My teachers all say that I am lazy because my work is not very good. They don't know that I find it very difficult to see what is written on the chalkboard, so I do not always know what to do in lessons.

I am a good reader and I manage well when we work from books. I think that I may need glasses, but I would hate to have to wear them. What can I do?

Gemma

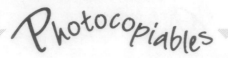
Sounds in space

Name _____ Date _____

▲ Use this sheet to write the names of your favourite five songs or tunes which you would send into space in a time capsule.

Photocopiables

Classified ads

▲ Turn these advertisements into classified ads using no more than 15 words including the seller's surname and telephone number.

FOR SALE

1988 Ford Escort with four doors.
The car has a stereo radio and a sunroof. It has been well looked after from new and has only had two owners.
The engine runs beautifully and the bodywork shows no signs of rust.
The car's MOT certificate runs out in October and it is taxed until November.
The car also has electric front windows and a tow bar.
Reasonable offers around £2000 considered.
Contact Louise Chadwick, 01509 466530

FOR SALE

Child's mountain bike. Ideal for 9- to 11-year-old. The cycle is an unwanted Christmas present and has hardly been used. It is in excellent condition.
The bike has 10 gears and a speedometer. It also has lights, and a frame bag is included.
£65 or near offer or will consider larger bicycle in exchange.
Contact Mr S. Douglas, 01896 873007

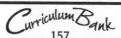

WRITING

INFORMATION TECHNOLOGY WITHIN WRITING

Main IT focus

The main emphasis for the development of IT capability within these activities is on communicating information, and in particular on word processing and desktop publishing. Indeed most of the activities in this book can involve word processing in some form or other. Where opportunities for IT have not been identified specifically, there may still be basic word-processing tasks that can be undertaken by some or all of the children. The activities which do have an 'Opportunities for IT' section are generally those which introduce different ways to use the word processor, or involve new skills.

Word processors

During Key Stage 2, children should be developing their confidence and competence to use word processing or desktop publishing packages. Many word processors now have basic desktop publishing features, such as the ability to import pictures, position and resize them on the page, and it may be possible to use a single piece of software for most writing tasks.

A key difference, however, between the two types of software is the way in which text is placed on the page. In a desktop publishing package, text is generally placed inside a frame which can be altered in size and shape; the text is automatically reformatted to fill the new shape. This provides a flexible way for children to organise text and pictures on a page and to experiment with different types of page design.

Children should already have a basic knowledge of the keyboard and should be given opportunities to develop some of the more sophisticated aspects of using a word processor or desktop publishing package. These should include learning how to:

▲ use more than a single finger/hand when typing, particularly when knowledge of location of letters is gained;
▲ separate and join text using the 'return' and 'delete' keys;
▲ move the cursor to a mistake and correct it without deleting all the text back to the mistake;
▲ scroll around the document using the mouse or cursor keys;
▲ select an appropriate font from a menu;
▲ change the size and/or colour of a font;
▲ underline a word or line;
▲ alter the style of a word or sentence, for example italics or bold;
▲ centre text using the centre command;
▲ use the tab key to create columns;
▲ align text so that it is left-aligned/right-aligned/fully justified, and reset this option;
▲ save and retrieve work from a disk, eventually unaided;

▲ print completed work unaided;
▲ use a spelling checker to check work;
▲ add a picture to a document, positioning it and resizing it.
 Higher order skills might include:
▲ altering the 'ruler' to change margins and set tab keys;
▲ adding page numbers;
▲ setting up a master page to create a consistent layout throughout a document;
▲ setting up a text style to use within the document.

It is important that children are shown how to use specific formatting commands such as tabs, indents and centring to position text instead of using the space bar. This ensures that text can easily be reformatted without deleting spaces. On some word processors the hidden codes used for tabs or returns (pressing the enter key) appear on the screen so that editing is made more obvious.

Some children will take a long time to enter text at the keyboard so it is important to ensure that the writing tasks are kept short. If parents or other adults are available, they can often be used for support, provided they have the relevant skills. It is important that the teacher, or other adults, is available to intervene as children are working to teach them new skills appropriate to the task being undertaken.

Children should also be given opportunities to originate their work at the computer keyboard rather than always writing it out longhand and simply using the word processor to make a 'fair copy' for their folder or display purposes. It is often appropriate for children to make their first draft at the keyboard, save it, print it out and then redraft it away from the keyboard, thus giving another child the opportunity to use the computer. They can then return later on to make any changes they have decided upon and format the final copy for printing.

Many of the activities suggest the use of word-processed files created in advance by the teacher for the children. Such activities reduce the necessity for text entry and can enable children to concentrate on a new language concept or skill, or on the more sophisticated word-processing commands used in editing, organising and presenting work for an audience. When such files are created, it is important to make sure that a backup is kept and where possible the 'master' file is locked against accidental overwriting when children save their amended version of the file.

Where activities such as sequencing involve moving text around the page, the use of the 'cut and paste' facility is helpful. Word processors differ in the way that they achieve this. Word processors which use a mouse allow children to highlight the text to be moved by dragging the mouse across it. It can then be 'cut' out of the text so that it is placed on a clipboard hidden in the computer's memory. The cursor is then moved to the new position and the text 'pasted' in the required place. On some word processors this can be achieved by simply dragging the highlighted text to the new position. This is called 'drag and drop'.

The grids on this page relate the activites in this book to specific areas of IT and to relevant software resources. Activities are referenced by page number, and bold page numbers indicate activities which have expanded IT content.

AREA OF IT	SOFTWARE	ACTIVITIES (PAGE NOS.)			
		CHAPTER 1	CHAPTER 2	CHAPTER 3	CHAPTER 4
Communicating information	Word processor	**16**, 17, **24**, 25, 26, 29, 32, 35, 36, 37, 40, 43, 44, 45, 46	50, 51, **53**, 56, 57, 60, 61, 62	67, 68, 69, 76, **78**, 81, 85, 87, 88, 89, 91, 92, 93	98, **100**, 101, 102, 104, 105, 106, 109
Communicating information	DTP	16, 18, 24, 32, 36, 40, 43	52, 53, 58, 60		**101**, 102, 108, 109
Communicating information	Art/Drawing	29, 32, 40, 43	52, **59**	73, 91	
Communicating information	Framework	32	53		
Communicating information	Multimedia	20, **31**, 32, 36, 37	56	**79**	106
Information handling	CD-ROM		51, 58		
Information handling	Branching database	**38**			
Information handling	Database		**63**		

SOFTWARE TYPE	BBC/MASTER	RISCOS	NIMBUS/186	WINDOWS	MACINTOSH
Word processor	Folio	Pendown Desk Top Folio	All Write Write On	Microsoft Word Kid Works 2 Creative Writer	Kid Works 2 EasyWorks Creative Writer
DTP	Front Page Extra Typesetter	Desk Top Folio 1st Page Pendown DTP	Front Page Extra NewSPAper	Creative Writer NewSPAper	Creative Writer
Framework		My World 2 Bookmaker		My World 2	Easy Book Story Book Theatre
Art Package		Revelation Kid Pix Splash	PaintSpa	Colour Magic Kid Pix 2	Kid Pix 2
Drawing Package	Picture Builder	Draw Poster	Picture Builder	ClarisWorks	ClarisWorks
Multimedia Authoring		Hyperstudio Magpie Genesis		Hyperstudio Illuminatus Genesis	Hyperstudio
Branching Database	Branch	RetReeval	Branch		
Database	Grass	Junior Pinpoint Find IT Key Note	Grass	Sparks Junior Pinpoint Information Workshop	ClarisWorks EasyWorks

WRITING

	MATHS	SCIENCE	HISTORY	GEOGRAPHY	D & T	IT	ART	MUSIC	RE
IMAGINATIVE WRITING	Using horoscopes to examine probability.	Studying weather for writing about weather in a project. Research on animals and their characteristics.	Researching historical figures.		Making books for younger children and for class library. Making dice and other solid shapes.	Use of word processor for text manipulation, drafting and editing.	Drawing character illustrations to accompany text. Making greetings cards. Drawing illuminated letters for prayers.	Adapting new lyrics to hymn tunes. Syllable clapping for haiku. Rhyme scanning.	Rewriting lyrics for hymns. Writing prayers. Researching biblical figures.
NON-FICTION WRITING	Collating results of questionnaires. Constructing flow charts of familiar activities.	Researching and verifying facts. Constructing a flow chart.	Telegrams and their use. Postcards from historical characters. Reading diary extracts from famous and historical figures. Researching and verifying facts.	Researching and verifying facts. Constructing a flow chart.	Finding recipes from home and writing them in chronological order.	As above.	Drawing a picture of an ideal room. Designing book covers. Producing programmes related to school events.		
LANGUAGE STUDY	Working out percentages of four-letter words used in a piece of writing.		Reading a story with a historical theme to emphasise importance of correct use of commas. History of dialects and language changes.	Researching dialect words; marking dialect areas on maps to show influences on English language.		As above.	Making a collage of questions. Designing a poster using exclamation marks.	Sounds and onomatopoeia.	
PERSUASIVE WRITING	Working out budgets for classified ads. Presenting collated information in graphs and tables.		Researching local places of interest.	Researching local places of interest.		As above.	Completing a drawing of a famous person.	Choosing favourite pieces of music.	